THE MAKING OF
GEORGE ORWELL

For E.F.A.

THE MAKING OF
GEORGE ORWELL

AN ESSAY IN LITERARY HISTORY

KEITH ALLDRITT

NEW YORK: ST. MARTIN'S PRESS

© Keith Alldritt 1969

First published 1969 by
Edward Arnold (Publishers) Ltd
41 Maddox Street, London W1
First published in
the United States of America in 1969
by St. Martin's Press Inc.
175 Fifth Avenue, New York, New York

Library of Congress Catalog Card Number: 69–17404

PRINTED IN GREAT BRITAIN
BY W & J MACKAY & CO LTD, CHATHAM

PREFACE

In preparing this book I have been greatly assisted by financial support from the Committee on Research of the Dean of Graduate Studies at the University of British Columbia. I also wish to thank my friend Sherman Paul for reading the manuscript and suggesting many major improvements in style and substance. To my wife Judith Morse Alldritt I am indebted for her interest, criticism and constructive suggestions at every stage of the writing.

K.A.

ACKNOWLEDGMENTS

The Publisher and author gratefully acknowledge the permission granted by Miss Sonia Brownell and Martin Secker & Warburg Ltd. for quotations from George Orwell's published works; Chatto & Windus Ltd. for an extract from *Culture and Society* by Raymond Williams; Gerald Duckworth & Co. Ltd. for an extract from *Image and Experience: Studies in a Literary Revolution* by Graham Hough; William Heinemann Ltd. for an extract from *English Journey* by J. B. Priestley; Macmillan & Co. Ltd. for extracts from *Essays on Literature and Ideas* by John Wain; Mr. Michael Yeats and Macmillan & Co. Ltd. for an extract from 'Under Ben Bulben' in *Collected Poems of W. B. Yeats*; the Trustees of the Estate of the late Lord Keynes and Macmillan & Co. Ltd. for an extract from *The Economic Consequences of the Peace* by Maynard Keynes; Routledge and Kegan Paul Ltd. for an extract from *Enemies of Promise* by Cyril Connolly; Martin Secker & Warburg Ltd. for an extract from *George Orwell: Fugitive from the Camp of Victory* by Richard Rees, and Sweet & Maxwell Ltd. for an extract from an essay, 'Outside the Whale' by E. P. Thompson in *Out of Apathy*.

Acknowledgements are also due to the following holders of American copyright who have kindly granted permission for the use of material controlled by them:

Brandt and Brandt Inc., N.Y. for extracts from *Burmese Days, Coming Up for Air, Down and Out in Paris and London* and *1984* by George Orwell; Columbia University Press for an extract from *Culture and Society* by Raymond Williams; Harcourt Brace and World Inc., N.Y. for extracts from *Collected Essays, Enemies of Promise, The Road to Wigan Pier, Keep the Aspidistra Flying, Road to Catlonia* and *Such, Such were the Joys* by George Orwell; William Heinemann Ltd. for an extract from *English Journey* by J. B. Priestley; the Macmillan Company, N.Y. for an extract from *The Economic Consequences of the Peace* by Maynard Keynes and *Under Ben Bulben* by W. B. Yeats, Copyright 1940 Georgie Yeats, renewed 1968 Bertha Georgie Yeats, Michael Butler Yeats and Anne Yeats; St. Martin's Press for an extract from *Essays on Literature and Ideas* by John Wain; Southern Illinois University Press for an extract from *George Orwell: Fugitive from the Camp of Victory* by Richard Rees; Sweet & Maxwell Ltd for an extract from R. K. Thompson's essay 'Outside the Whale' from *Out of Apathy*; The University of Nebraska for an extract from Graham Hough's *Image and Experience*.

How dreary swift, with naught to travel to,
Is Time? I cannot bite the day to the core.

Edward Thomas

Ich bin aufgewachsen als Sohn
Wohlhabender Leute. Meine Eltern haben mir
Einen Kragen umgebunden und mich erzogen
In den Gewohnheiten des Bedientwerdens
Und unterrichtet in der Kunst des Befehlens. Aber
Als ich erwachsen war und um mich sah
Gefielen mir die Leute meiner Klasse nicht
Nicht das Befehlen und nicht das Bedientwerden.
Und ich verliess meine Klasse und gesellte mich
Zu den geringen Leuten.

Bertolt Brecht

1

The literary career of George Orwell coincides almost exactly with the two decades of the thirties and the forties. His first book was published in 1933 and from then on his work appeared regularly until his premature death in January, 1950. Each of these decades appears to us now as a distinct and clearly defined entity in the recent social and political history of England. The thirties, in particular, have been identified long since and our feelings about them are very well organised. We remember these years, above all, as the most painful phase of the economic dislocation following the first World War. They are the years of economic depression and of widespread unemployment, heralded first by the Wall Street crash of 1929 and then again by the financial and political crisis in England in 1931. They are the years that marked the rise of Fascism abroad and the tendency towards appeasement and indecision at home. They are the years of contending ideologies and also of paralysis, not only in political and intellectual life but in the national life as a whole. They are the years that we have learned to patronise if not to scorn.[1] The forties also have their distinctive character, though

[1] The customary attitude to the thirties is established as early as 1940 in Malcolm Muggeridge's *The Thirties* (London, 1940). Julian Symons's *The Thirties: A Dream Revolved* (London, 1960) is a far more thoughtful book; it gives a much better sense of the life of the decade, particularly the intellectual life. Nevertheless, Mr. Symons's attitude to his subject, twenty years on, is also one of clear, albeit regretful, condemnation. Censure is also the dominant feature of other books which treat of this decade, such as Ronald Blythe's *The Age of Illusion* (London, 1963) and *The Baldwin Age*, ed. John Raymond (London, 1960).

it is one that is less susceptible to ready-made descriptions and judgments.[2] We think of this decade mainly as a time of action and achievement. The years of the second World War are still remembered and cherished, particularly by their own generation, as a time of heroic endeavour. And the unequivocal victory of the Labour Party at the election of 1945, together with the social changes that were subsequently legislated, still appears as a similarly decisive if less colourful moment in English life. As we look back upon the forties in memory or newsreels or photographs, it is the general shabbiness of the people and of the country itself that is the most striking feature and that most clearly distinguishes these years, and also the thirties, from the decade of the fifties, in which for a great majority in England austerity and deprivation were to give way to an ever increasing prosperity. It is this shabby England of depression, war and austerity that provides the setting for Orwell's novels. And it is the social and political issues of these twenty years that provide the themes of all his writings, imaginative and discursive alike. Certainly this is the customary view of him. And as far as it goes, it is a correct one. Nevertheless, it is also a very partial view, for it ignores much that is important in his work. Above all, and this is one of the major contentions of this essay, it ignores precisely those qualities that make Orwell's writings worthy of our continuing attention. For it is not primarily as social commentary or as political thought that his books are valuable to us. And the use of terms such as socialist or Trotskyist to characterise his writing is unhelpful. These are at best preliminary definitions of his position, definitions which are not conducive to an accurate discussion of his particular achievement. Insofar as the works of George Orwell continue to have value for us, it is a value which, for the sake of the necessary emphasis, must be called literary. Furthermore, their literary value is of a very special kind. With the possible exception of *Nineteen Eighty-Four*, Orwell created no valuable work of literary art; rather his contribution was to literary culture. Which is to

[2] There is already, however, a tendency to regard the forties as "period"; see *The Age of Austerity*, ed. Michael Sissons and Philip French (London, 1963) and also J. Maclaren-Ross, *Memoirs of the Forties* (London, 1965).

say that in order to understand his particular achievement, we must again refer his *oeuvre* to its historical context, but specifically to its context in literary history. During the twenty years in question the literary history of England does not have such clear outlines as the social and political history, nor does it lend itself so easily to broad summary. It is true, of course, that there is a literature which has come to be regarded as distinctively of the thirties, a literature characterised by a somewhat self-conscious engagement with ideological issues and created by young men who were at that time just beginning to become known as writers. The names that spring most immediately to mind are W. H. Auden, Stephen Spender, Christopher Isherwood, Louis MacNeice and Graham Greene. Nevertheless, it would not be denied that the writing of the greatest literary value produced during the thirties came from other poets and novelists who were not native to the decade. After all, during these years W. B. Yeats was still writing, T. S. Eliot was beginning his *Four Quartets* and in 1939, after some seventeen years of work on it, James Joyce published his *Finnegans Wake*. The main importance of the thirties as far as literary history is concerned is the fact that these years mark the continuation and the climax of the literary movement which began around the time of the first World War, the movement which we have recently become accustomed, as a result perhaps of our realisation that it is now over and our sense of being distanced from it, to identify and to name. We call it symbolism or more particularly, and in order to stress its affiliation with certain French writers of the late nineteenth century, most especially Baudelaire, Rimbaud and Mallarmé, *le symbolisme*.

Some general propositions about symbolism, necessarily crabbed though they must be, are an indispensable preliminary to any attempt to discuss the character of Orwell's work. For only when we relate his books to the profoundly influential aesthetic which formed their background can we properly understand and judge them.[3] The symbolist background accounts in

[3] Hitherto, published discussion of Orwell has tended to consider him more as an isolated figure. There have been eight book length studies of his work. The majority are by writers who were personally acquainted with him, but all eight are concerned principally with

3

great part for Orwell's failure as a creative literary artist; it also throws into relief his particular and interesting contribution to literary culture. In the portion of this essay that is devoted to Orwell's novels, I shall try to show how his failure as a novelist derives chiefly from his misguided efforts to write in accord with the symbolist manner, misguided because the assumptions of symbolism were intellectually and temperamentally uncongenial to him. The symbolist techniques that he endeavoured to use were thoroughly incompatible with his real concerns as a novelist, that is to say with the stories that he wanted to tell and the effects upon the reader that he wanted to achieve. Orwell did not succeed in completely extricating himself from the, to him, harmful influences of symbolism until after 1939 when the first phase of his career as a novelist was over. And when in the middle of the forties he returned to fiction and wrote *Animal Farm* and *Nineteen Eighty-Four*, it was not with the novel as such that he concerned himself, but rather with other species of the genus of prose fiction, such as the allegorical fable and the utopia —forms that were more resistant to the strong influences of Joyce, Proust and D. H. Lawrence.

Orwell's gradual disengagement from the symbolist outlook is also a theme of his non-fictional writings. These form the part of his *oeuvre* which seems to me the most important and with which I shall be chiefly concerned. With the exception of his six novels, Orwell's prose works all relate to each other, form a clearly discernible whole and should, if they are to be properly appreciated, be read as a piece. The three volumes published

---

Orwell the individual and with the biographical context and significance of his writings. These studies in order of publication are: John Atkins, *George Orwell* (London, 1954); Laurence Brander, *George Orwell* (London, 1954); Christopher Hollis, *A Study of George Orwell* (London, 1956); Richard Rees, *George Orwell: Fugitive From the Camp of Victory* (Carbondale, Illinois, 1961); Richard J. Voorhees, *The Paradox of George Orwell* (Purdue University Studies, 1961); Edward M. Thomas, *Orwell* (Edinburgh, 1965); George Woodcock, *The Crystal Spirit, A Study of George Orwell* (London, 1967) and B. T. Oxley, *George Orwell* (London, 1967). There is also a British Council pamphlet on Orwell by Tom Hopkinson. In subsequent references to these works I shall cite merely the author's name and the page number.

4

during the thirties, *Down and Out in Paris and London*, *The Road to Wigan Pier* and *Homage to Catalonia*, together with the sequence of essays which Orwell wrote during the forties, all coalesce to form one work of autobiography. The value of this work is twofold. It is first of all a record of one of the most painful periods of English experience as one articulate and responsible man underwent it. And here I am not thinking primarily of Orwell's conscious involvement in such public concerns as unemployment and the Spanish Civil War, but rather of the way his prose reveals his continuing struggle to achieve, in terms of his own individual consciousness, a moral confidence in the face of the moral uncertainty of the time. His autobiography is the history of his efforts to make a personality, a selfhood, which will allow of relationships that are morally and emotionally satisfactory. And the idea of a proper selfhood which he comes to propose is one not only different from that cultivated by the symbolist writers and emulated by the many literary intellectuals who admired them, but also quite original in terms of the modes of English personality recognisable at that time. Equally distinctive, inevitably, is the language in which the autobiography is written. The particular quality of this language, which is interesting both historically and in itself, is the second reason that the autobiography continues to be of value to us.

At its most mature in the later portions of the autobiography, this style is distinguished by its directness, its lively movement and its assimilation of some of the idiom and the raciness of common speech. There is in Orwell's writing a vitality and a cogency that are seldom to be found in the work of his contemporaries. These are the qualities of language which form his contribution to English literary culture of recent times. By the term literary culture I wish to denote the way language is used not only as the medium of literary art but also as the medium for all forms of written communication. The literary culture is best discerned in the particular types and in the quality of the prose that it produces. For it is in prose that the conditions and the level of literate intercourse are most readily observed. As far as twentieth-century prose is concerned, it is noteworthy that we are not strongly conscious of who the best prose writers are. Orwell, in fact, is one of the very few names that are likely to come to mind. Certainly this is not an age which has been greatly distinguished for its prose, and this is perhaps a symptom of the general debilitation of literary culture which has so often been remarked. By Orwell's time the decline of the literary culture was well under way. Insofar as the written language was informed at all by the literate sensibility, it was informed by the Bloomsbury sensibility, one that expressed itself in precious and mannered language of very limited usefulness. Much more influential was the heavy mechanical jargon of the social scientists and psychologists which Orwell protested against so strongly in his essay "Politics and the English Language". Above all, there was a lack of energy in the use of the language, a lack which manifested itself in passive constructions, lumbering latinate sentences, clichés, tonal banalities and that general inattention to words with which we are still familiar. It is in terms of this particular state of literary culture that Orwell's endeavour to write a living style must, both in its achievement and in its quite patent limitations, be judged. Literary culture is involved in the processes of historical change; and any given phase must, if it is to be understood at all, be placed in historical perspective. This is particularly true of the phase during which Orwell was at work. For then, perhaps more than at any other time, the achievement of the major literary artists—because of its particular nature—contributed little to the general literary culture. Orwell, indeed, enlivened English writing only insofar as he succeeded in dissociating himself from the assumptions of the great writers of the first quarter of the century. That is to say, his autobiography as well as his fiction must be sited in its proper relationship with symbolism.

The word symbolism I intend as a synecdoche. For though the writers who established the most seminal ideas about literary art in the early decades of this century, and who exerted a strong influence upon Orwell (Joyce, D. H. Lawrence, Eliot, Yeats, Proust), may all, without the word being laden with a burden greater than it can usefully bear, be described as symbolists, we must go on to say that the ethos which they created was sustained and extended by other developments in the intellectual life as distinct and as different as Freudian and Jungian analysis and the intuitionism of G. E. Moore. In rehearsing some of the

6

obvious characteristics of British symbolism during the years of *l'entre deux guerres*, I am trying merely to establish, however rudimentarily, what were some of the most prominent assumptions about literary art at the time Orwell began writing. The metaphor which commends itself as the most helpful in such an undertaking is the one which Edmund Wilson employed as the title of his pioneering study of symbolism, that of Axel's Castle. It is particularly useful in relation to a discussion of Orwell because, as I shall be showing, his work contains several passages which are reminiscent of Villiers de l'Isle-Adam's play. This is not to suggest that the influence was a direct one. As Richard Ellmann remarks in his introduction to Arthur Symons's *The Symbolist Movement in Literature*, "Since 1899 the French symbolists have steadily affected even writers who have not read them. . . ."[4] Mallarmé and those who surrounded him at the famous Tuesday gatherings in the Rue de Rome came to have such a pervasive influence upon the literary life of England that a writer of Orwell's generation could be touched by it and yet have no first hand knowledge of its origins.

The role of Arthur Symons in this diffusion of the symbolist aesthetic was extremely important. As Ellmann suggests, his book is the most obvious thread linking the French symbolists of the latter decades of the last century with the British symbolists of the early decades of the present one. Written at a time when Symons was an intimate of W. B. Yeats and dedicated to him as "the chief representative of that movement in our country", the book also impinged strongly on the career of T. S. Eliot. "I myself owe Mr. Symons a great debt;" Eliot wrote in 1930, "but for reading his book I should not, in the year 1908, have heard of Laforgue or Rimbaud; I should probably not have begun to read Verlaine; and but for reading Verlaine, I should not have heard of Corbière. So the Symons book is one of those which have affected the course of my life."[5] Understandably, Eliot was interested primarily in the poets of the movement rather than in Villiers de l'Isle-Adam, whose reputation

[4] Arthur Symons, *The Symbolist Movement in Literature*, with an Introduction by Richard Ellman (New York, 1958), i.
[5] T. S. Eliot, Review of *Baudelaire and the Symbolists* by Peter Quennell, *Criterion*, IX (January, 1930), 357.

rests upon his work as a dramatist and short story writer. But for Symons himself there was no more important contribution to symbolism than that of Villiers. He, it is claimed, was at the centre of things, "greatly loved, ardently admired by that inner circle of the men who have made modern French literature, from Verlaine to Maeterlinck . . ." And it is to Villiers that Symons, in his influential book, ascribes the distinction of "creating a new form of art, the art of the symbolist drama, and of Symbolism in fiction".

Of all the plays of Villiers, *Axel* is the best known. And it continues to deserve attention today, not so much on account of its intrinsic literary worth, but rather because it reveals more clearly than any other individual work the premises upon which symbolism, French and English alike, is based. The attitudes of its hero, clearly endorsed as they are by his author, are *the* symbolist attitudes, ones which have informed the work of the most creative literary talents of our century. First and foremost, of course, is Axel's famous contempt for the external world and his insistence that consciousness alone is real; "Oh! le monde extérieur! Ne soyons pas dupes du vieil esclave, enchaîné à nos pieds dans la lumière, et qui nous promet les clefs d'un palais d'enchantements, alors qu'il ne cache, en sa noire main fermée, qu'une poignée de cendres!"[6] Some brief summary of the play will perhaps be helpful here in further developing the implication of these words. Axel is a young German nobleman of ancient lineage living in his ancestral castle deep in the Black Forest. He is attended only by a few aged retainers and by Master Janus, a Rosicrucian and cabalist. The crisis of Axel's life, as it is presented in the play, is created by the temptation to forsake his secluded life of mystical contemplation and to enjoy worldly experience. To Axel's castle there come two visitors who, each in a different way, try to induce him to give up his isolation and "live". Commander Kaspar, a courtier and worldling, seeks to persuade him to look for the great treasure which legend says is buried on Axel's estate and then to return with him to enjoy the various pleasures of court life. Axel's highly developed sensibility is grossly offended by

[6] *Oeuvres Completes de Villiers de L'Isle-Adam* (Paris, 1923), pp. 263, 264.

this suggestion, and he challenges Kaspar to a duel and kills him. Yet Kaspar's visit has nevertheless and against his will excited Axel's interest in the external world. He finds himself unable to undergo the final initiation into the occult mysteries at the hands of Master Janus. And the second temptation represented by the arrival of Axel's distant kinswoman, Sara, is less easily resisted. Brought up in a French convent, Sara has also renounced the spiritual life by refusing to take the final vows of a nun. She and Axel fall in love. They find the hidden treasure and dream of travelling together through the world and of experiencing all that life has to offer. But at the end of the play, Axel returns to his contempt for life and convinces Sara that the actual experiences would be inferior to the dreams of them that they have shared, and he proposes that they kill themselves. Life in the external world has nothing to offer, he maintains, which would not be but a vulgar travesty of the supreme moments of consciousness which they have already known: "Accepter, désormais, de vivre, ne serait plus qu'un sacrilège envers nous-mêmes. Vivre? les serviteurs feront cela pour nous."[7]

These words of Axel's, particularly the last sentence cited, have come to be very famous ones. And this is because they express, with a lack of equivocation that is quite memorable, something central to the symbolist outlook—an over-riding concern with the internal psychic life of man and a corresponding disdain towards the phenomenal world outside. It is the view which determines the characteristically symbolist choice of subject matter for literary art. The correspondence is shown very clearly in, for instance, Mallarmé's account of his art as "une poétique très nouvelle que je pourrais définir en ces deux mots; peindre non la chose, mais l'effet qu'elle produit." And T. E. Hulme made virtually the same emphasis when, in a lecture before his fellow "imagists", he claimed that modern art "no longer deals with heroic action, it has become definitely and finally introspective and deals with expression and communication of momentary phases in the poet's mind."[8] Imagism,

7 *Ibid.*, p. 261.
8 T. E. Hulme, "A Lecture on Modern Poetry" in *Further Speculations*, ed. Sam Hynes (Minneapolis, 1955), p. 68.

9

signifying a group of poets who met very occasionally but very enthusiastically during the ten years between 1908 and 1918 to discuss poetic principles and to publish anthologies, is but one of the symptoms of the growth of the symbolist aesthetic in England. (The member of the group most closely in touch with the French poetry of the nineties was F. S. Flint.) But though we may point to the evocative, non-discursive imagist poem as one type of symbolist poetry, it is not to any avowedly imagist work that we shall go in order to observe how this particular concern with consciousness manifests itself most impressively and most influentially in a work of art. For that we must turn to T. S. Eliot's *The Waste Land* of 1922. The particular state of mind which this most famous of modern poems is concerned to evoke may be described as that of spiritual impotence. The poem is a monologue in which the speaker, the prophet figure Tiresias, gives expression to his consciousness, to his train of thought and feeling, which subsumes the people, the voices, the sounds, the objects and the townscape of the modern world. These external phenomena are not recorded for their own sake, nor with the logic of description. They are there as evocations of the speaker's *état d'âme*. They are the images of his state and they appear and recur not in a logical order, but in accord with the movement of consciousness itself. The phenomena are there as they are in order to suggest Tiresias's emotion, his feeling of spiritual aridity in all its despairing movement and detail. The poem is the perfect illustration of Eliot's theory about "the only way of expressing emotion in the form of art". This, it will be remembered, involves "finding . . . a set of objects, a situation, a chain of events which shall be the formula of that particular emotion; such that when the external facts, which must terminate in sensory experience, are given, the emotion is immediately evoked". And though this idea, like the several other symbolist devices for the rendering of consciousness, has come to be a bit too familiar to us, it retains some interest in that it shows quite explicitly the characteristic symbolist emphasis in dealing with the relationship between the objective and subjective worlds.

Symbolist art involves, of course, more than the rendering of consciousness for its own sake. A much more distinguishing feature is its preoccupation with those moments of consciousness in which a reality above and beyond that which the senses may perceive is apprehended. "A symbol," wrote W. B. Yeats, "is indeed the only possible expression of some invisible essence, a transparent lamp about a spiritual flame." The desire to gain and to express glimpses of such a transcendental reality explains in great part the fascination which mysticism and magic have held for symbolist writers. The symbol is, in fact, in one of the many senses which they attached to this all important word, very much like the sign of the magus.[9] It serves, in Yeats's words again, "to call down among us certain disembodied powers whose footsteps over our hearts we call emotions". And in no other modern poet is this concern with the occult more readily observable than in Yeats himself. The mysticism which informs the poetry of T. S. Eliot is one which is registered in terms of more orthodox categories. In *Four Quartets*, surely the most superb symbolist poem in English, there are expressed not merely the processes of an individual psyche but also, and more importantly, the psychic state in which confident realisation is made of a transcendent order, pattern and harmony, of a time-less world beyond the world of time. We may also remark that the chief theme of D. H. Lawrence's novel *The Rainbow* is similar to that of Eliot's poem. For the aim of the heroic *lebensfähige* Brangwens is to create "a new knowledge of Eternity in the flux of Time". And although Lawrence's art as a whole is very obviously founded upon assumptions quite different from those of the symbolists, his concerns and his literary techniques are often very reminiscent of theirs. He shares their preoccupa-tion with states of feeling and with transcendence. And the way he uses the symbol or image to evoke them in, say, *The Fox* or *St. Mawr* is quite in keeping with the Yeatsian definition which I cited earlier. Lawrence also shares the symbolist preoccupa-tion with history. As Frank Kermode has reminded us in his *The Romantic Image*, a fundamental tenet of symbolism is that at some point in the history of western civilisation there occurred a

[9] No one single, comprehensive and convincing definition of the symbol is readily available. Professor Lehmann has listed eight dis-tinct interpretations of the word to be found among the symbolist writers; see A. G. Lehmann, *The Symbolist Aesthetic in France 1800–1895* (Oxford, 1950), pp. 306, 307.

bifurcation of human consciousness which resulted in a degeneration in the quality of art, culture and life itself. This is the assumption that lies behind Yeats's question: "had not Europe shared one mind and heart until both mind and heart began to break into fragments a little before Shakespeare's birth?"[10] And it is the same assumption which is present in T. S. Eliot's concept of "the dissociation of sensibility" (even though Eliot's definition of the crucial historical moment is different from that of Yeats). Lawrence propounds essentially the same view in the lengthy interpretations of history that are to be found in "Study of Thomas Hardy" and some of the chapters of *Twilight in Italy*. As might be expected, Lawrence also had his own particular idea of the turning point. But his basic view is very much the symbolist one. Like Yeats and Eliot, he identifies a moment in history at which both the unity of the individual mind and the unity of society become broken and which heralds a subsequent impoverishment of life, that very impoverishment which stands as the prime *donnée* of symbolist thought and art.

Nevertheless, it remains true that there is much that distinguishes Lawrence from his symbolist contemporaries. He has less in common with Yeats, Joyce and Eliot than they have with each other. Above all, his sense of what Yeats called "the disembodied powers" is not, like theirs, confined to what we ordinarily think of as the spiritual.[11] In this regard, much more typical of the symbolist aesthetic are the assumptions underlying the fiction of James Joyce. The "epiphanies" which Stephen Dedalus, in the early novel *Stephen Hero*, thought "it was for the literary man to record" were, we recall, "sudden spiritual manifestations', "the most delicate and evanescent of

[10] "The Trembling of the Veil" in *The Autobiographies of W. B. Yeats*, Anchor Books (New York, 1958), p. 129.

[11] This complex and interesting matter is discussed in Mark Spilka's article, "Was D. H. Lawrence a Symbolist?" *Accent*, XV (Winter, 1955). Mr. Spilka also returns to the problem in an early chapter of his *The Love Ethic of D. H. Lawrence*. It will suffice here to say that what chiefly distinguishes Lawrence's art from that of the symbolists are his values in judging the quality of consciousness. Nevertheless, his central concern is with the inner life, and many of his literary techniques reveal very distinctly his relationship with the dominant literary aesthetic of the time.

moments". The desire to capture such delicacy and evanescence also accounts for the symbolist interest in music, an interest which manifests itself in the exuberant verbal experimentation in *Finnegans Wake* and more soberly in the title and the techniques of *Four Quartets*. And if Stephen Dedalus's much discussed theory of literary art is representative, so also is his idea of the role of the artist. His contempt for his environment, his indifference to the social and political issues of the modern world, his denial of the claims of family, church and country, his eventual self-imposed exile from modern life and his single-minded devotion to art and to aesthetic theory, are all characteristic of the symbolist position. So too is his disdain for the day of the rabblement and his identification with the traditions of honour and aristocracy represented by the heroes of Ireland. In all these respects he bears a close resemblance not only to Axel but also to each of the major symbolist writers, as each has presented himself *in propria persona*; that is to say, to Joyce himself, whose surrogate Dedalus is (however qualified the endorsement may be), and to Yeats and to Eliot. Yeats's disdain for modern civilisation and his corresponding admiration for an earlier, more heroic time are well known. Nowhere are they more clearly articulated than in the penultimate stanza of "Under Ben Bulben" where Yeats enjoins the Irish poets who will follow him to:

> Scorn the sort now growing up
> All out of shape from toe to top
> Their unremembering hearts and heads
> Base born products of base beds.
> Sing the peasantry and then
> Hard-riding country gentlemen.

As C. M. Bowra has suggested, there is considerable justification for regarding symbolism as "an aristocratic reaction against the insurgent tide of democratic opinions".[12] Certainly the ideas of Yeats, Joyce and Eliot about culture, communication and proper social relationships (including the relationship between writer and reader) all bespeak the same aloofness and hauteur that we associate with Villiers de l'Isle-Adam himself. And like

[12] C. M. Bowra, *The Heritage of Symbolism* (New York, 1961), p. 12.

him, they have all been much at pains to invoke their lineage as a means of self-definition. This symbolist cult of the aristocratic must appear to us as something forced and self-conscious. Such attitudes are very obviously contrived, just as contrived and fabricated as the working-class persona adopted by a Brecht or an Orwell. Nevertheless, this propensity of the modern writer to wear a mask or, as I think we may more accurately say, to reconstitute the self, is one of the most striking features of the phase of literary culture with which we are here concerned. And it is not peculiar to the symbolist writers (though they do have their own particular idea of a proper selfhood); for it is clearly as much a psychological necessity, as much an indispensable part of literary activity for Orwell as it is, say, for T. S. Eliot.

The reasons for this urgent concern with self-definition are many and complex. But one comparatively obvious one, and one that is also an important condition of George Orwell's career, involves the easily appreciable change that took place during the first quarter of the present century in the relations between the writer and his predominantly middle-class society. We may say that the particular antagonism between artist and society dating back at least to the Romantic period and culminating, in the opinion of some, in the trial of Oscar Wilde had abated by the time of the first World War. And, of course, it was precisely at this moment that symbolism started to establish itself as the pre-eminent literary aesthetic in England. This *détente* in the old antagonism between artist and society seems mainly attributable to the loss of certitude on the part of the middle classes themselves, to that breakdown in confidence of which the first World War was both a consequence and an intensification. Few in 1919 had a better sense of the economic, social and intellectual direction of European life than Maynard Keynes. And this is how he describes the historic moment in his first hand account of the treaty of Versailles:

> We are thus faced in Europe with the spectacle of an extra-ordinary weakness on the part of the great capitalist class, which has emerged from the great triumphs of the nineteenth century, and seemed a very few years ago our all powerful master. The terror and personal timidity of the individuals of this class is now so great, their confidence in their place in society and in their

necessity to the social organism so diminished, that they are the easy victims of intimidation. This was not so in England twenty-five years ago, any more than it is now in the United States.[13]

This sudden failure of nerve on the part of the middle class clearly affected literary art in at least two important ways. In the first place it accounts for the disappearance of the bourgeois from literature as a serious antagonist to the artistic vision and to the artist. The major writers of the time have not had an Homais or even an Edwardian Wilcox to deal with. In *The Waste Land*, as in the fiction of Joyce and Lawrence, the bourgeois himself is very much devitalised and, in the final instance, more a pitiable figure than a redoubtable opponent. And secondly, we may say that this new uncertainty affected the writer himself, both in his idea of himself and in his idea of his function. For neither through participation in nor even in opposition to the life of his class could the writer achieve a confident selfhood. If modern literature is concerned with the unviability, the super-annuatedness of the old forms of middle-class personality, it is also greatly, almost obsessively, concerned with new definitions of what constitutes the artist. And if it treats of the lack of firm assumptions in human relationships generally, it also bespeaks, quite unmistakably, the uncertainties in the particular relationship between the artist and his audience. These two facts of modern experience explain in great part the particular preoccupation with self, the particular introvertedness, of the symbolist artist. The studied impersonality which is frequently attributed to Joyce and to Eliot we may see as but one expression of this lack of certitude. And the donning of the aristocratic persona is a symptom of the very same malaise. Given what T. S. Eliot, in his well-known review of Joyce's *Ulysses*, called "the immense panorama of futility and anarchy which is contemporary history",[14] the symbolist has assumed archaic forms of

[13] J. M. Keynes, *The Economic Consequences of the Peace* (London, 1919), p. 222. It may be remarked that the style of this brief passage from Keynes's polemic, itself one of the most important prose works of the twenties, constitutes an interesting historical comparison with Orwell's manner of writing.

[14] T. S. Eliot, "Ulysses, Order and Myth", *The Dial*, November, 1923, 480–483.

personality in order to detach himself from the drift of life in his time. He has withdrawn into himself and sought an awareness of the valuable in the past and in literature itself rather than in actual experience. And only those who have been prepared to follow him into such obscure regions have been able to appreciate his art. Even among such readers there are those who resent this lack of involvement in contemporary experience and who feel that a more direct and more obvious engagement with the present is indispensable to a proper discharging of the artistic function. This is what Graham Hough seems to be suggesting, for instance, in his unfavourable comparison of the symbolists with the Romantic poets. He writes:

> In reading *The Prelude*, Keats's *Odes* and the two *Hyperions*, or *Prometheus Unbound*, one is conscious of thought that profoundly affects the poet and his fellows, actually being worked out in the process of writing the poetry. One who has read these works, even if he has read nothing else, has felt much of the force and pressure of the age. A reader of the characteristic modern work—shall we say *The Waste Land*, *Hugh Selwyn Mauberley* and *Ulysses*? will have experienced something far more peripheral, something that cannot take him, as the work of the Romantic poets can, close to the very centre of the time.[15]

This criticism of symbolist art rests on two presuppositions: that symbolist works do not let us feel "the force and pressure of the age," and that valuable art does do exactly this. Obviously both are very debatable. As far as the first is concerned, it is surely undeniable that the particular nature and concerns of symbolist art are determined by the conditions of the age. Though it is also true that they do not have the direct, clear-cut relationship demanded by the second assumption. For, insofar as the phrase "the force and pressure of the age" is intelligible, the demand seems to be that the art of an age should clearly reflect the developments, presumably the social, political and intellectual developments and so forth, of the age. For the moment it is not to my purpose to become further involved in such an argument, even though this essay as a whole is in one respect very much concerned with it. All I want to establish at

[15] Graham Hough, *Image and Experience: Studies in a Literary Revolution* (London, 1960), p. 75.

present is that the argument exists. It is the very argument to which, I think, Frank Kermode is referring when, in his book on the symbolists, he speaks of "the unformulated quarrel between the orthodoxy of Symbolism and the surviving elements of an empirical utilitarian tradition which we are assured is characteristically English."[16] And it is precisely this argument which is at the centre of everything that Orwell wrote. His autobiography and his fiction are interesting chiefly as a continuing attempt to find a viable alternative to the symbolist assumptions that dominated the literary life of his time.

Orwell, I want to show, began to write as an adherent of symbolism. Like others of the thirties generation, he was powerfully affected by the literary othodoxy that had been established a generation earlier, in the nineteen-tens. But what was peculiar to him was the urgency of his subsequent desire to free himself from symbolist categories and to explore possibilities of altogether different modes of feeling and selfhood. For Orwell the writer this also entailed a new sense of the writer's function and a new relationship and tone with the reader. These pre-eminent features of his intellectual life are to be observed in the three books and the thirty or so essays comprising the autobiography. These works, as I have said, will be my main concern; though I shall also want to consider the extent to which Orwell's gradually acquired ideas of literary culture served him when, towards the end of his life, he resumed the writing of fiction. Orwell's discursive prose has a certain intrinsic value of its own. But insofar as it relates a continuing effort to formulate counterproposals to the major literary assumptions of the age, it also provides a particularly clear and striking perspective upon that age. As a first step in establishing this perspective it will be useful to describe Orwell's intellectual situation as a writer beginning in the thirties. And there is no better way of doing this than to consider briefly his attempts during those years to write symbolist novels.

[16] Frank Kermode, *Romantic Image* (London, 1957), p. 152.

2

In what was otherwise a very favourable account of Orwell's work, Q. D. Leavis dismissed out of hand the novels that he wrote during the thirties. "Mr. Orwell must have wasted a lot of energy trying to be a novelist," she wrote. "I think I must have read three or four novels by him and the only impression those dreary books left on me was that nature didn't intend him to be a novelist."[17] This is a view which most of Orwell's critics have shared, even if they have not expressed it with such confident forthrightness. And it is a view which seems to me quite un-challengeable. My only reasons for renewing the discussion are that the changes in theme and outlook which occur over the four early novels help to illuminate the changes in Orwell's emotional and intellectual life that are set down in the auto-biography and also that the nature of the failure of the novels is connected with a further theme of the autobiography—Orwell's estrangement from the most influential ideas in the literary culture of his time.

Orwell obviously had neither the intricate sensibility nor the creative energy of the true novelist. Even at its best his work is heavily derivative. And this deficiency is compounded by his failure to follow his true masters. Though he sought continually to emulate the symbolists, his categories of thought and feeling were completely different from theirs. The tradition of fiction which alone was compatible with his temperament and which conceivably he might have revivified had it continued at all vital or had he felt more confidence in it, was the essentially

[17] Q. D. Leavis, "The Literary Life Respectable," *Scrutiny*, IX (September, 1940).

English tradition represented by Dickens, Gissing and Wells. And if any one of the modern aesthetics was suitable to his talents, it was certainly not that which was nurtured in the Rue de Rome, but rather its despised alternative, naturalism. Zola's novels were an early influence on Orwell and they were clearly an enduring one. It is to Zola, for instance, that Orwell turns in his first book, *Down and Out in Paris and London*, when, as an inexperienced writer whose own distinctive style has yet to crystallise, he senses the weakness of his descriptive and evocative powers. "I wish I could be Zola for a little while," he remarks, recalling the hectic activity of the Parisian hotel kitchens, "just to describe that dinner hour." And throughout Orwell's writings references to Zola recur, as do those to the now largely forgotten novelist who tried to transplant naturalism in England, George Moore. In the essay on Rudyard Kipling, for example, Moore is mentioned together with Gissing and Hardy as representative of the serious and commendable art which was beyond Kipling's powers. And if we can agree with John Atkins that the long list of writers which "Tubby" Bowling in *Coming Up For Air* remembers reading are "the authors whom Orwell read and to varying degrees enjoyed when he was a young man",[18] we will find Moore taking his place beside Wells ("who made the biggest impression on me") as a writer whom Orwell definitely admired. "I read George Moore's *Esther Waters* and liked it," he recalls; and the impact of the book on him would seem to have been quite strong, for one of the characters in *Coming Up For Air*, Elsie Waters, is obviously, and in more than name alone, modelled upon Moore's heroine.

In his essay "Why I Write", composed towards the end of his life, Orwell recollected his boyhood ambition "to write enormous naturalistic novels with unhappy endings, full of detailed descriptions and arresting similes . . .". "And in fact," he goes on to say, "my first completed novel, *Burmese Days*, which I wrote when I was thirty but projected much earlier, is rather that kind of book." Because it is true to the naturalist idea of fiction, which was so long an established part of Orwell's mentality, *Burmese Days*, first novel though it is, stands as one of his more successful fictions. Granted there are many other influences at

[18] Atkins, p. 283.

work in the book, more English influences such as that of Dickens, it is nevertheless essentially a naturalist work. Zola's influence is specific as well as general. For not only can it be said of Orwell in *Burmese Days*, as a recent critic has said by way of characterising Zola's fiction, that "preoccupied less with characters than with their characteristics, he is finally interested less in temperament than in milieu",[19] it has to be further remarked that Orwell explains the career and fate of his hero in the typically naturalist terms of heredity and environment.

The title of the novel has an ironic intention. For the two words which might seem at first to suggest some agreeable memoirs, a volume of pleasant reminiscences of life in Burma, actually denominate the story of a man's suffering and destruction as a result of his involvement with Burma and with his fellow Englishmen who rule it. Orwell's hero, John Flory, is an English timber merchant based at the remote British outpost in Kyauktada in Upper Burma. He is a man of some intelligence and sensitivity; and the story tells of his foredoomed endeavour to maintain civilised and humane standards in the face of his fellow Englishmen, in whom life in Burma elicits at the very best a bungling philistinism and at the worst a pathological cruelty. Flory's struggle is as much with the material as with the social environment. Orwell himself in *The Road to Wigan Pier* remarked that the scenery is the real subject matter of his first novel, and certainly the long descriptions of the Burmese landscape, wild life and seasons are the most memorable passages in the book. Furthermore, the setting is also the most important force in the novel. In his early days in Burma Flory had loved the landscape; indeed his love for it never completely disappears. But as he grows older, he also comes to see it as something which is weakening his will to adhere to his idea of a proper life. On the one occasion when he makes an effort to leave Burma and to escape the moral horror, the boredom and brutality of Anglo-Indian life he finds that he lacks sufficient resolution. "Eight years of Eastern life, fever, loneliness and intermittent drinking had set their mark upon him." After this failure to implement his desire to return to civilisation, Flory is henceforth as much a captive of his environment as any of the Rougon-Macquart, and

[19] Harry Levin, *The Gates of Horn* (New York, 1963), p. 339.

like so many of them, doomed to destruction by it. His captivity is also defined in the specifically materialist terms characteristic of the naturalists:

> It was one of those moments when one becomes conscious of a vast change and deterioration in one's life. For he had realised that in his heart he was glad to be coming back. This country which he hated was now his native country, his home. He had lived here ten years, and every particle of his body was compounded of Burmese soil.

If Burma has set its mark on Flory, so also has heredity; though Orwell's use of this element of naturalist doctrine is such that it has symbolic force rather than meaning in straightforwardly genetic and physiological terms. Flory's difficulties in life, explains the narrator, "had begun in his mother's womb when chance put the blue birthmark on his cheek." This disfigurement accounts for the timidity and nervousness which are the chief causes of Flory's destruction. Throughout his life he is ill at ease socially, and in Burma particularly so; for here his intelligence and perceptiveness make him even more of a marked man. His relationship with the other Englishmen in Kyauktada is strained because he cannot share their imperturbable confidence in the rightness of the British Raj. The political order which to them is sacrosanct is to Flory a racket; while they feel nothing but contempt for the Burmese, Flory takes a lively and admiring interest in the local culture, and while they avoid all contact with Asiatics, Flory finds his only confidant in the Indian civil servant, Dr. Veraswami. The consequence of all this is that Flory has minimal contact with his fellow Europeans; "he had learned to live inwardly, secretly, in books and secret thoughts that could not be uttered." "But it is a corrupting thing to live one's life in isolation," remarks the narrator, who also makes it clear that this corruption stems from Flory's innate inability, symbolised by the ugly birthmark, to relate easily and happily to other people, a tendency which is fatally aggravated by the particular milieu in which he finds himself in Burma. The novel is an account of human aspiration gradually but inexorably destroyed by the force of circumstances. And Orwell himself is quick to demand for Flory the same sort of compassion that we feel for, say, Gervaise in *L'Assommoir*: "It

22

is not the less bitter because it is one's own fault to see oneself drifting, rotting, in dishonour and horrible futility, and all the while knowing that somewhere within one there is the possibility of a decent human being."

But the desired effect is not achieved. Despite Orwell's close adherence to the naturalist formula, the reader is unable to grieve for Flory and his fate, or in any way to become compassionately engaged with him. And this is because Flory, like most of the other characters in the book, is unliving and artificial. We remember him merely as the decent, sensitive imperialist, in the way we remember some of the others as the drunken imperialist, the sadistic imperialist, the stuffy imperialist who comes out with Latin tags, and so on. They are all as obviously contrived as the story in which they figure. And the plot is one of the very worst features of the book; throughout we are conscious of the narrator flagrantly manipulating events. At one point Flory is about to propose marriage to Elizabeth Lackersteen; but Flory's continuing loneliness is necessary to the thematic import of the novel and so an earthquake, of all things, is introduced to prevent the proposal from taking place. And at the very moment when Flory is supporting the nomination of Dr. Veraswami as the first Asian member of the English Club, the body of an Englishman murdered by the Burmese is brought in, creating a wave of anti-Burmese feeling and robbing Flory of the opportunity of taking a clear-cut moral stand. This sort of sensationalism can be attributed in part to Orwell's inexperience; but it also derives from his determination to have a strong plot in the manner of the nineteenth-century novelists. The influence of Dickens in particular is very strong in the novel. As John Atkins has observed, the summing up of the future careers of the leading characters in the last chapter is very much in the manner of *David Copperfield*.[20] And Dickens has clearly aided in the creation of the one memorable character in the book, the Burmese magistrate U Po Kyin, who by his cunning schemes and machinations to become the first Oriental admitted to the Club brings about the downfall of both Flory and Veraswami. The obese magistrate's villainy is so radical and thoroughgoing that he is also, like some of Dicken's villains,

[20] Atkins, p. 269.

comic. And like them he has readers who abstract him from his fictional context and admire him for his own sake. "U Po Kyin," says Laurence Brander, with perhaps a touch of exaggeration, "is a tremendous figure and Orwell's first claim to be mentioned among the satirists."[21]

But U Po Kyin notwithstanding, the novel as a whole does not come to life. And this is because it strikes us as a set of literary exercises which are not unified into a satisfactory artistic statement. Admittedly some of these individual set pieces are excellently done. Here, for instance, is a Georgian nature sketch, which though more robust and less subtly responsive than Edward Thomas's or those in D. H. Lawrence's first novel *The White Peacock*, still shows Orwell's considerable powers in observing and evoking the external world.

> It was the beginning of the short winter, when Upper Burma seemed haunted by the ghost of England. Wild flowers sprang into bloom everywhere, not quite the same as the English ones, but very like them—honeysuckle in thick bushes, field roses smelling of peardrops, even violets in dark places of the forest. The sun circled low in the sky, and the nights and early mornings were bitterly cold, with white mists that poured through the valleys like the steam of enormous kettles. One went shooting after duck and snipe. There were snipe in countless myriads, and wild geese in flocks that rose from the jeel with a roar like a goods train crossing an iron bridge. The ripening paddy, breast high and yellow, looked like wheat. The Burmese went to their work with muffled heads and their arms clasped across their breasts, their faces yellow and pinched with the cold. In the morning one marched through misty incongruous wildernesses, clearings of drenched, almost English grass and naked trees where monkeys squatted in the upper branches waiting for the sun. At night coming back to camp through the cold lanes, one met herds of buffaloes which the boys were driving home, with their huge horns looming through the mists like crescents. One had three blankets on one's bed, and game pies instead of the eternal chicken. After dinner one sat on a log by the vast campfire, drinking beer and talking about shooting. The flames danced like red holly, casting a circle of light at the edge of which servants and coolies squatted, too shy to intrude on the white men and yet

[21] Brander, p. 79.

edging up to the fire like dogs. As one lay in bed one could hear the dew dripping from the trees like large but gentle rain. It was a good life while one was young and need not think about the future or the past.

Despite the suggestion of poeticising contained in a phrase like "countless myriads", this is in general an impressive piece of prose. And it gives the promise of Orwell's considerable powers as a writer, as distinct from those of a novelist. Throughout his career Orwell was able to evoke milieu freshly and with a detailed accuracy; but he was unable to bring the same qualities to the rendering of character, human relationships or states of feeling. And herein lies his basic failure as a novelist. He was never able to present human beings in anything other than set and rigid categories; his characters are just derived literary formulas. And this explains in part that excessive intrusion of the authorial voice which mars all his novels. Since Orwell is unable to invest his people with life, it is not through characters or their interaction or their development that the vital issues which he wants to raise can be treated. The result is that Orwell himself feels it necessary to step forward and establish a direct man to man relationship with the reader. At one crucial point in *Burmese Days*, to take just one of many possible examples, when he is attempting to present Flory's consciousness of the horror and the isolation of his life in Burma, narrative peters out, Flory is abandoned and forgotten and Orwell himself speaks to us about his own experience in Burma:

You are free to be a drunkard, an idler, a coward, a backbiter, a fornicator; but you are not free to think for yourself. Your opinion on every subject of any conceivable importance is dictated to you by the pukka sahib's code.

In the end the secrecy of your revolt poisons you like a secret disease. Your whole life is a life of lies. Year after year you sit in Kipling-haunted little Clubs, whisky to the right of you, *Pink-un* to the left of you, listening and eagerly agreeing while Colonel Bodger develops his theory that these bloody Nationalists should be boiled in oil. You hear your Oriental friends called "greasy little babus", and you admit, dutifully, that they *are* greasy little babus. You see louts fresh from school kicking grey-haired servants. The time comes when you burn with hatred for your own countrymen, when you long for a native rising to drown their Empire in blood.

Taken by itself this passage could easily be mistaken for an excerpt from one of the autobiographical volumes. And many such passages recur in all of his novels. In each of them we have the feeling that Orwell has set out to write a novel, to transmute his experience in such a way that it may be communicated with the impact of art, only to give up and turn to reporting and to moral commentary. His greatest difficulty as a novelist was the rendering of consciousness. This was because he himself lacked that indispensable self-confidence of the artist which allows him to regard and to dramatise his consciousness in its various aspects as representative of the civilisation of his time. Orwell was without this confident egocentricity, and that is why he is at his best as an autobiographer and essayist speaking, usually quite tentatively, for himself alone. This difficulty was compounded when he proceeded to try to broaden his own vision, which was essentially that of a Dickensian caricaturist, by experimenting with the devices of symbolism, which were as alien to him as they were to that English tradition of which he was the inheritor. The uneasy collocation of Dickens and naturalism which we find in *Burmese Days* will have its even more unsatisfactory counterparts in the novels which follow. John Atkins tells us that even in the last days of his life Orwell was studying Conrad and still "meditating on the interaction of the English and the continental mind".[22] This interaction is an important theme in Orwell's life as it is described in the autobiography, and in the novels we see it developing in specifically literary terms. Orwell was obviously impressed by the literary art which was founded on those assumptions which we have associated with the name of Axel. His references to Baudelaire, Proust, Joyce, Yeats, Eliot and D. H. Lawrence are invariably admiring and respectful; and he himself tried to emulate their methods. But at the same time a part of his mind adhered to that other idea of literature, so long established in him, which involved the presentation of life in terms of externals and in terms of a friendly and generous relationship between writer and reader such as we associate

[22] Atkins, p. 65.

with Dickens or Arnold Bennett. The irreconcilability of these two views, both in fundamentals and in the specifics of literary practice, does much to explain Orwell's renunciation of the novel form halfway through his career.

The first of the experimental works is *A Clergyman's Daughter*, Orwell's second novel and one which in later life he made every effort to supress. Here the most striking instance of Orwell's unfortunate determination to assimilate symbolist techniques is the third chapter, which is a dramatic tableau, a phantasmagoria peopled by the down and outs who gather in Trafalgar Square by night. Atkins has suggested that in this passage Orwell "was probably influenced by Joyce";[23] and I think we can go on to say more specifically that it is a pale imitation of the Circe episode in *Ulysses*. Orwell's intention, it would seem, is to convey the sensation of crazed despair as it is experienced by the starving. But with all its phantom characters, its "monstrous winged shapes of Demons and Archdemons", and the black mass which it contains, the tableau remains a literary exercise which may intrigue us but certainly does not engage us in the way that the original does. The full power of Joyce's influence upon Orwell is to be seen in a later novel. In *A Clergyman's Daughter* it is confined to this one chapter. A much more pervasive influence is that of D. H. Lawrence; for Orwell's second novel seems to have had not only its title suggested by Lawrence's fine *novelle, Daughters of the Vicar*, but much of its subject matter too.[24] Orwell's heroine, like Lawrence's, is the daughter of an Anglican vicar whose parish is situated in a recently industrialised town where the great majority of the people are either indifferent to religion or nonconformists and uninterested in the Church of England. The Reverend Charles Hare, like Mr. Lindley in *Daughters of the Vicar*, is from a good family and has aristocratic tastes and attitudes. He is unable to reconcile himself easily to the genteel poverty and to the social

[23] Atkins, p. 87.
[24] For an account of Orwell's enthusiastic admiration for Lawrence, see Rayner Heppenstall, *Four Absentees* (London, 1960).

27

isolation which are his lot as the vicar of a small Suffolk town. And the working people from the local sugar beet refinery, who ignore him, he views with contempt. ("It is simply abominable how these people take it upon themselves to behave nowadays—abominable! But there you are, you see. That is the kind of thing that we are exposed to in this delightful century. That is democracy—*progress*, as they are pleased to call it.") Like his Laurentian counterpart, the Reverend Hare withdraws as much as possible from the unfriendly world around him. And the practical day to day management of the vicarage, the church and the parish affairs falls upon his daughter, Dorothy. It is she who must face the creditors, struggle to save halfpennies, deliver the parish magazines, visit the sick and organise fund-raising pageants and plays.

A not unattractive woman of twenty-seven, Dorothy Hare is reminiscent of some of Lawrence's female characters in that she is frightened by the idea of being loved by a man. "To be kissed or fondled by a man—to feel heavy male arms about her and thick male lips bearing down upon her own—was terrifying and repulsive to her. Even in memory or imagination it made her wince. It was her especial secret, the especial incurable disability that she carried through life." But Orwell does not give us, as Lawrence so often does, the story of a woman's awakening to love and a new awareness of life and selfhood. In *The Daughters of the Vicar* Louisa Lindley manages, by a conscious choice, to reject the way of life commended by her family, a way which allows, at best, only the sterile sensations of social superiority. And by committing herself to the young miner Alfred Durant, she finds her awareness no longer restricted to the categories of class, but suddenly broadened so that she becomes conscious of other and richer possibilities in human relationships. But for the heroine of Orwell's book there is no such discovery. Indeed her life comprises a loss of exhilaration and purpose rather than a gain. For after a period of amnesia, she finds that she has lost the religious faith which, practised rigorously and with many acts of self-mortification, had previously been the foundation of her life.

Loss of faith is the chief theme of the novel. It is also an issue which Orwell frequently deals with in his essays. But though it is obvious that the matter was of importance to Orwell as an idea, we can only conclude from *A Clergyman's Daughter* that it was not a profound personal experience for him, or at least that, if it was, he was unable to convey the experience in fictional terms. What is so tremendously impressive about Lawrence's *Daughters of the Vicar* is that it does transmit to us, particularly in the scene where Alfred and Louisa embrace for the first time, the sensation of new life. The failure of *A Clergyman's Daughter* is that the spiritual aridity which comes over Dorothy is not real to us. It is not established as a feeling; it is only there in Orwell's commentary. "And given only faith, how can anything else matter?" he asks. "Your whole life is illumined by that sense of purpose. There is no feeling of futility, no Baudelairean *ennui* waiting for unguarded hours." The reference to Baudelaire suggests that Orwell is here trying to purvey the fashionable idea of what the specifically modern consciousness is, an impression which is reinforced when we read elsewhere of "the corrupting *ennui* that lies in wait for every modern soul".

Dorothy's sudden loss of faith, her sense of God being withdrawn from her life, seems to be intended as an example of "waste land" experience. But neither her faith nor her loss of it really comes across as felt experience. The whole situation is but an *idée reçue*, something which has literary and intellectual significance for Orwell but with which he is not in sympathetic emotional contact. Though he obviously felt obliged to follow in the steps of Lawrence and Baudelaire and Eliot, he was not at home in their world. This failure to stick to his last and his propensity to be intimidated into accepting the idea of the real held by the dominant literary movement of the time, rather than viewing the world in his own terms, makes his novels appear superficial, even sometimes silly.

That Orwell himself did not feel fully at ease in treating Dorothy's spiritual crisis is shown by the fact that he only deals with it at the beginning and at the very end of the book. Once Dorothy is afflicted with amnesia, the spiritual problem can be conveniently shelved until the concluding pages. The book then becomes a picaresque novel and Orwell is able to write about more congenial matters. This middle portion of the book is the best thing in it, though except for the presence of the main characters, these pages might strike us less as fiction than as further excerpts from Orwell's own picaresque autobiographies. When Dorothy partially comes to herself again after the sudden violent access of amnesia, she finds herself in a shabby part of London where she is taken up by a group of Cockneys with whom she goes hop-picking in Kent. The subsequent descriptions of the Kent countryside, of the Cockney hop-pickers and of the conditions in which they live are all memorable as reportage in a way that the book as a whole is not memorable as a novel.

Reportage of a more purposeful and critical sort is introduced in the descriptions of a later phase in Dorothy's wanderings when, having left the hop-fields and having spent some time without money among the down and outs of London, she obtains, through the sudden intervention of a relative (and the plot of this second novel is even more improbable than that of the first), a job in a third-rate private school in a London suburb. Orwell's description of Ringwood House, its pupils and the travesty of education which it provides and of its vulgar, money-grabbing proprietor Mrs. Creevy are well done, probably because they are derived from Orwell's own first-hand experience.[25] And it is surely an anger born of personal experience that motivates Orwell's many criticisms of the school. "Such schools exist, like shops, by flattering their customers, and if a parent wanted his child taught nothing but cat's-cradle and the cuneiform alphabet, the teacher would have to agree rather than lose a pupil." "So long as schools are run primarily for money, things like this will happen."

The whole situation at Ringwood House together with this element of crusading criticism which it elicits from Orwell is again reminiscent of Dickens, and so also is the character of Mrs. Creevy who, at once the battleaxe and skinflint, dominates this area of the novel. And Orwell himself is explicit about his affiliation to the tradition in which he writes. "The whole atmosphere of the place," he remarks, "was so reminiscent of

[25] It is known that Orwell himself taught in a private school. But it seems likely that the influence of D. H. Lawrence is also at work in this portion of the novel. Dorothy's realisation that it is impossible to treat a classroom of children as individuals recalls the experience of Ursula Brangwen in *The Rainbow*.

those dreary little private schools that you read about in Victorian novels." When he adheres to this particular tradition, Orwell's writing is alive and interesting; when he feels compelled to counterfeit experience, his work becomes flat. This also explains the unsatisfactoriness of the major characters of his novels. Their autobiographical origins are, as critics have often pointed out, quickly recognisable. "Flory was clearly to some extent Orwell as he imagined that he might have been had he stayed in Burma," remarks Christopher Hollis.[26] And even Dorothy Hare in her "horror of sex manifested in a ceaselessly nagging conscience" is, as Tom Hopkinson has observed, "the representative of a strong side of his nature"[27] (a side which it was obviously less disturbing to dramatise in terms of a female character). But though these characters and their circumstances issue from important experience on the part of their author, they are unsatisfactory and unconvincing. It is as though throughout the thirties, at the same time that he was trying to understand himself in his straightforwardly autobiographical volumes, he was also experimenting from novel to novel in trying to fit his experience into known literary categories. Having tried unsuccessfully in his first two novels to interpret himself in Zolaesque and then in Laurentian terms, he turned in his third to the procedures of James Joyce.

In the opinion of Gordon Comstock, the hero of *Keep the Aspidistra Flying*, ". . . Lawrence was all right, and Joyce even better before he went off his coconut." The judgment is flippantly worded; but the intensity of Joyce's influence on Comstock's creator is clear enough.[28] Orwell's third novel is his attempt at the portrait of the artist. Like Stephen Dedalus, Comstock struggles to free himself from the despised life around him. He pities and rejects his family and all that they stand for, lives in a way they find unsatisfactory and spends much of his time

[26] Hollis, p. 37.
[27] Hopkinson, p. 19.
[28] Orwell's account of the impact of Joyce's work upon him is to be found in the essay "Inside the Whale".

developing and explaining his own position to a sympathetic intellectual friend, Ravelston. And in the same way that we are shown Dedalus transmuting various moments of his experience into a villanelle, we also see Comstock piecing together a similarly undistinguished poem.[29]

In Orwell's novel the autobiographical element is as strong as in its Joycean prototype. Like Orwell himself Comstock has a strong desire to go down and out. The deep need to escape from the life and dictates of bourgeois respectability which Orwell in *The Road to Wigan Pier* recorded as one of the most important experiences in his own life is also an obsession with Comstock. "He wanted to go down, deep down, into some world where decency no longer mattered." "He liked to think that beneath the world of money there is that great sluttish underworld where failure and success have no meaning; a sort of kingdom of ghosts where all are equal." And like Orwell, Comstock has his origins in the Scottish middle class: "Gordon Comstock was a pretty bloody name, but then Gordon came of a pretty bloody family. The 'Gordon' part was Scotch, of course. The prevalence of such names nowadays is merely a part of the Scotchification of England that has been going on these last fifty years." The irritation discernable here reminds us of Orwell's dissatisfaction with his own Scots origins. As we know from *The Road to Wigan Pier,* he regarded the vaunting of Scots associations and even visits to Scotland as particularly loathsome prestige emblems. Comstock is also an Orwellian self-portrait in as much as his family is ordered by the same sort of shabby, poverty-stricken gentility described by Orwell in the autobiographical essay "Such, Such Were the Joys". Indeed Orwell remarking *in propria persona* upon Gordon's education as a poor boy in a school for the rich is very reminiscent of Orwell commenting in the essay upon his own boyhood. "Probably the greatest cruelty one can inflict upon a child is to send it to a school among children richer than itself. A child conscious of poverty will suffer snobbish agonies such as a grown-up person can scarcely imagine."

[29] It is worth noting that Comstock's poem was published over Orwell's name in *The Adelphi* of November, 1935.

But the similarity between the author and hero is easily demonstrable without adducing such external evidence. For the novel is written in such a way that it is often very hard to distinguish between Orwell's authorial comments and the musings of Gordon Comstock. In the following passages, for instance, in which we are told how aspiration to class and to gentility reduces the vitality and the quality of middle-class life, we are not at all sure, given the context, whether we are sharing the thoughts of the character or of his creator:

> It was not poverty but the down-dragging of respectable poverty that had done for them. They had accepted the money-code, and by that code they were failures. They had never had the sense to lash out and just *live*, money or no money, as the lower classes do. How right the lower classes are! Hats off to the factory lad who with fourpence in the world puts his girl in the family way! At least he's got blood and not money in his veins.

And again:

> That was what it meant to worship the money-god! To settle down, to Make Good, to sell your soul for a villa and an aspidistra! To turn into the typical bowler-hatted sneak—Strube's 'little-man'—the docile little cit who slips home by the six-fifteen to a supper of cottage pie and stewed tinned pears, half an hour's listening in to the B.B.C. Symphony Concert, and then perhaps a spot of licit sexual intercourse if his wife "feels in the mood!" What a fate!

The deadening effect of serving the money-god is really the chief theme of *Keep the Aspidistra Flying*. The account of Comstock's career as an artist is foisted onto this and not endemic to it. The passages that are there to present Gordon as a poet are often characterised by hackneyed meaningless statements ("He drove his mind into the abyss where poetry is written") and have none of the energy to be found in the descriptions of Comstock's and/or Orwell's horror at the lifelessness and materialism of modern bourgeois civilisation. It is as though Orwell starts off to make the portrait of himself as an artist but after the first few chapters, loses interest in this original purpose and realises, as does his surrogate at the end of the novel, that "the whole concept of poetry was meaningless to him now". Once again Orwell has patterned his work upon a derived idea of the novel which bears no relationship to the experience that he really wants to treat.

Though Orwell has made Comstock resemble Stephen Dedalus in many superficial ways, the two characters are truly alike in only one respect; they are both repelled by the way their fellow-men live and taking disgust as their premise, build upon it an intellectual position and a practical policy with such wilful and cerebral doggedness as to frighten their acquaintance. In this regard it is interesting to note that one of the most thoughtful readers of Joyce has found it revealing to consider the similarity between Stephen and Sherlock Holmes. "Holmes and Watson," writes Hugh Kenner, "epitomise humanity dissected into ratiocinative violence and sentimental virtue, the latter avid of absorbtion into the former."[30] Gordon Comstock is also interested in the famous detective. "*Sherlock Holmes* was his favourite of all books, because he knew it all by heart." And this is a taste shared by Orwell himself; in *Down and Out in Paris and London* he tells us that in his hungriest days in Paris he would retire to bed and read the *Memoirs of Sherlock Holmes*. And in his essay on "The Art of Donald McGill" Orwell shows himself aware of a dualism in literature and experience which is not far different from the one defined by Mr. Kenner; "It comes up again and again in endless variations, Bouvard and Pecuchet, Jeeves and Wooster, Bloom and Dedalus, Holmes and Watson." Comstock is clearly Orwell's experiment at adopting the position of "ratiocinative violence". He is the arrogant young intellectual, contemptuous in his sensibility, proud in the isolation which it entails, without any bond of sympathetic feeling with the life going on around him. The relentlessly inhuman logic and the fundamental contempt with which Holmes pursues his cases and Dedalus his aesthetic are employed by Comstock against his society. His Dr. Watson is Ravelston, who because he is left-wing is impressed by the sheer radicalism of Gordon's tirades, but who (because he is also quite wealthy) is unable to feel the same separation from, the same horror of society as Gordon:

[30] Hugh Kenner, *Dublin's Joyce* (Boston, 1962), p. 170.

And now they were off upon their favourite subject—Gordon's favourite subject, anyway; the futility, the bloodiness, the deathliness of modern life. They never met without talking for at least half an hour in this vein. But it also made Ravelston rather uncomfortable. In a way, of course, he knew . . . that life under a decaying capitalism is deathly and meaningless. But this knowledge was only theoretical. You can't really *feel* that kind of thing when your income is eight hundred a year.

By the end of the book neither Gordon nor his creator is able to continue to feel this way. The loneliness which is the result of this form of moral and intellectual scrupulousness is more than either of them can bear. Orwell himself suddenly and quite unconvincingly resolves the tension between artist and society with the rather platitudinous plot device of imminent extramarital paternity; and Gordon, who began as a ravening Dedalus, ends as a potential Bloom.

At the conclusion of the novel when Gordon surrenders his original position, when he recants his *non serviam* to the money-god, Orwell still identifies himself with his hero and with some relief endorses his decision: "He was thirty and there was grey in his hair, yet he had a queer feeling that he had only just grown up. It occurred to him that he was merely repeating the destiny of every human being. Everyone rebels against the money-code and everyone sooner or later surrenders." "After all he did not lack vitality, and that moneyless existence to which he had condemned himself had thrust him ruthlessly out of the stream of life." Admittedly the heavy irony with which Orwell views Comstock's future career "in homburg hat of the correct gutter-crawling pattern, neatly shaved and with his hair cut short", provides some transition between the relish of Comstock's thoroughgoing rejection of society and the commendation of his sudden acceptance of a life within it. Nevertheless there is still an embarrassing contrast between the Orwell/Comstock of the opening chapters and the Orwell/Comstock of the penultimate chapter who writes like this: "Our civilisation is founded on greed and fear, but in the lives of common men the greed and fear are mysteriously transmuted into something nobler."

The fact that Gordon's rehabilitation in the service of the money-god is imposed upon the plot rather than deriving naturally from it is the greatest fault in the novel. And it is clear that it stems from an imperfectly resolved tension in Orwell's own mind; the tension between the intellectual's desire to be true to his finest perceptions and the desire to enjoy fellowship with the people around him—desires which in modern times have been notoriously incompatible. "The stream of life" is a phrase which haunts the minds of Orwell's surrogates, Flory as well as Comstock. Both feel thrust out from it and both, sooner or later, try to return to it. Flory fails and perishes of his isolation. Comstock, on the other hand, succeeds in remaking his perceptions and is, in some sense, saved. This new resolution of the old problem is precisely what is significant about the later book. *Keep the Aspidistra Flying*, however unconvincing and inexpert as a novel, is of interest because it shows Orwell's first fumbling efforts to free himself from the idea of the literary intellectual that prevailed in his time.

Sir Richard Rees, in his interesting and informative account of Orwell's career, has suggested that "there was a striking change of mood in 1936", the year in which this third novel was published.[31] And when we come to look at the autobiographies we will see that between *Down and Out in Paris and London* and *The Road to Wigan Pier* (this last also appeared in 1936) there occurs a change of outlook on Orwell's part which parallels the one observable in *Keep the Aspidistra Flying*. It represents his renunciation of the sort of literary asceticism inherent in symbolist attitudes, and a movement toward the view expressed in one of the later essays where Orwell suggests that one condition of "being human" is "that one does not push asceticism to the point where it makes friendly intercourse impossible". Orwell moves from a lonely intellectual individualism to a realisation of the possibilities of community, to a sense of alliance which will find expression in political terms in his becoming a socialist. It is a movement away from the proud, lonely cultivation of sensibility to an acceptance of involvement in society. "Temperamentally he is egotistic and romantic, intellectually he is clearly aware that the egotist and the romantic must go." These words help to define Orwell's change of attitude, though they were, in fact,

[31] Rees, p. 78.

used by H. G. Wells about himself when speaking of a similar experience in his own life.[32]

Wells, like Dickens, was as we know from the many references to him in the essays an important experience for Orwell as a young man. And it is perhaps because of Orwell's own sudden wholehearted social concern that the resurgent influence of Wells is so strong in his last thirties novel, *Coming Up for Air*. In this book the hero is not a Dedalus, a Raskolnikov, a Holmes or a Comstock but their contrary, a Bloom. George Bowling is middle-aged, lower middle-class, closely if painfully involved with family and friends, and inextricably caught up in the social and economic system. Orwell is clearly much more at home with this sort of hero than he was with his Dedalus figure. He is able to stay the distance of the novel and to sustain a smoother and more convincing thematic development. Nevertheless even here Orwell has not managed to free himself completely from modish symbolist techniques. He still tries, albeit perfunctorily, to treat of internal experience, and this time after the manner of Marcel Proust.

From Proust come the basic situation of the novel and many details. The story of George Bowling, the rather stout, undistinguished insurance agent with wife and two children living on a jerry-built housing estate in the Thames Valley, is a crude and comically over-simplified version of the story of Marcel in *A la Recherche du Temps Perdu*. George is also in search of time past, that is to say the way of life which he had known during his boyhood in the small market town of Lower Binfield. And like Marcel he is subject to the promptings of the involuntary memory. At the very start of the novel, when he is walking down the Strand and thinking about the imminence of war, Bowling catches sight of a newspaper stand proclaiming "King Zog's Wedding Postponed". As these words move through his mind, he finds himself thinking of two old men who had sung in the church choir when he was a boy. He remembers the psalm "that

[32] Quoted by Bernard Bergonzi in *The Early H. G. Wells* (Toronto 1961), p. 121.

37

has the bit about Sihon king of the Amorites and Og the king of Bashan" and this, in Proustian fashion, brings back his childhood. The words on the news-vendor's placard operate on Bowling in the same way that the scent of the madeleine dipped in tea did upon Marcel. Bowling also proceeds to comment upon this strange experience in the same way as his original, but at considerably less length.

> The past is a curious thing. It's with you all the time. I suppose an hour never passes without your thinking of things that happened ten or twenty years ago, and yet most of the time it's got no reality, its just a set of facts that you've learned, like a lot of stuff in a history book. Then some chance sight or sound or smell, especially smell, sets you going, and the past doesn't merely come back to you, you're actually *in* the past. It was like that at this moment.

There are also in the novel numerous passages in which Bowling, very conscious of his middle age, offers in his own chatty way Proustian reflections on the passage of time and also states of consciousness as they are affected by time. "When you're very young you seem to suddenly become conscious of things that have been under your nose for a long time past. Things around you swim into your mind one at a time, rather as they do when you're waking from sleep."

Unignorable though the Proustian influence may be, it is not dominant. Orwell in *Coming Up for Air* has a new confidence in his fictional purpose; and derived symbolist ideas do not here, as in the earlier novels, disrupt the book. The proposed emphasis upon the changes in the state of mind of the hero quickly becomes subordinate to the presentation of change in the society of which he is a part. The evocation of the momentous changes in English life in the first three decades of the present century is quite well managed and makes this book the most distinguished of Orwell's early novels.

The life and times of George Bowling comprise three distinct phases. First there is the Edwardian boyhood in a quiet Oxfordshire market town which is presented convincingly and unsentimentally. This portion of the novel, describing the life of a none too prosperous shopkeeping family, is obviously indebted to

Wells, above all to his *History of Mr. Polly*. (And Hardy seems to have helped with some of the details of country life.) The one feature of the Edwardian time which, in Bowling's view, differentiated it from what followed was "a feeling of security, even when they weren't secure. More exactly, it was a feeling of continuity. All of them knew they'd got to die, and I suppose a few of them knew they were going to go bankrupt, but what they didn't know was that the order of things could change." "Individually they were finished, but their way of life would continue. Their good and evil would remain good and evil. They didn't feel the ground they stood on shifting under their feet."

The first World War brings an end to this sort of stability and initiates what Bowling, in something of a Laurentian phrase, terms "a ghastly flux." Bowling finds himself removed from the grocer's shop and, after some service in France, an officer with the ludicrous responsibility of guarding twelve tins of bully beef on the Cornish coast. For Bowling, whose typicality is insisted upon throughout, the war deranged not only his individual attitudes and expectations but also the whole social and moral order of England. "If the war didn't happen to kill you, it was bound to start you thinking. After that unspeakable idiotic mess you couldn't go on regarding society as something eternal and unquestionable, like a pyramid. You knew it was just a balls-up." The society of fear to which Bowling returns after the war is the one which Orwell had already described in *Keep the Aspidistra Flying*; but in this later novel the horror and the vulgarity of it are documented more extensively: the fear of losing a job, the commuter's round, the shoddy new suburban housing estates which sprawl over the countryside and bury Lower Binfield, the cheap clothes, the mass-produced furniture and food, and the raving ideologies which preach hatred—hatred which stems from the all-pervasive fear symbolised by the dive bombers sweeping over London as Bowling moves around the city like Bloom wandering around Dublin.

Bowling is Orwell's best essay in character creation. At times he is very credible; his distinctively modern speech, for instance, is especially well put down. Nevertheless, he remains at the last far too much of a type. Orwell obviously cannot rest content with his man of the people. Bowling (who is the first and only character presented from the first person point of view) sometimes has opinions which strike us as implausible. He has an articulateness which seems unlikely in an insurance salesman who is continually boasting of his lowbrow status and interests. ("I'm what you might call a typical Boots library subscriber." "I'm the ordinary middling kind that moves on when the policeman tells him." "God knows at normal times I don't have many interests that you wouldn't expect a middle-aged seven pound a weeker with two kids to have.") The very fact that Bowling is made to assert his averageness in this way suggests a certain defensiveness on the part of his author, a defensiveness which is perhaps understandable seeing that Bowling is prone to apocalyptic visions of the imminent war and is revealed to have considerable political insight and concern. We come to feel that this average "seven pound a weeker" is just a Bloomlike disguise for the attitudes and interests of George Orwell. Or, to put it another way, Bowling is an unsatisfactory character in that he is too much the incarnation of a socialist intellectual's dream—the man of the people who is politically conscious and thoughtful. Bowling is the very antithesis of the somnolence and apathy which Orwell found in England upon his return from the Spanish Civil War and which he so deplored in the final paragraph of *Homage to Catalonia*, which was published just a year before *Coming Up for Air*.

Orwell's ideological purpose (and of course he has such a purpose, even though it is not easily categorised under some standard "ism") works in other ways to weaken the credibility of Bowling. Though his speech, as I have said, is that of a living man and though in an incident such as his shyness at being seen with flowers in his hand we are momentarily aware of a living character, Bowling is too frequently reduced to and insisted upon as a sociological specimen. All the facts of his life are that bit too appropriate to his social station. He has the right sort of wife (frigid, pennypinching and whining), the right number of children (two), the right sort of house and the right sort of car. Furthermore he is too precisely a member of his generation. His age and year of birth are repeated throughout the novel so that we may not forget what a good sample figure this is to represent the change brought about by the social, economic and moral

40

revolution of the first quarter of this century. As well as the central character, the story itself is rigged here and there so that Orwell may make his point about the fear and the hatred underlying both the capitalist system and the relations between modern nations. There is, for instance, the incident of the bombs which are accidentally dropped on Bowling's home town during an R.A.F. bombing practice. George is made to comment that a newspaper subsequently reported that the authorities had found the bomb "disappointing" because it accounted for only three deaths. This incident is a gross example of Orwell's tendency to sacrifice probability in order to make an ideological point.

But despite these defects, *Coming Up for Air* has, especially in comparison with Orwell's earlier novels, some good things in it. It marks a great advance in his skill as a novelist and shows his realisation of who his true masters in the art of fiction are. He has seen at last that the writers who were fashionable in the intellectual circles of the thirties—Proust, Joyce and Lawrence—are of little help to him in saying what is in him to say. And he has found a more suitable model in Wells, though it cannot be denied that Wells's crude sociologising exerts an unfortunate influence by confirming a certain obtuseness in Orwell's sensibility. Although Orwell's novels are but a footnote to the history of the modern novel, a casualty of the symbolist aesthetic in fiction, it is still a question whether Orwell, had he lived longer, might have refined his social insights and restrained his tendency toward obtrusive and often crude commentary, and thereby made some more impressive contribution to the novel form. That the form continued to interest him is known from his intention in the closing days of his life "to make a break from his former polemical, propagandist way of writing and to concentrate upon the theme of human relationships."[33] But Orwell was to be denied such an opportunity, and *Coming Up for Air* marks his last venture with the novel. The year that it was published the second World War broke out. And Orwell's experience of the war and of the cold war which followed was to draw his interest away from the novel and direct it towards different species of the genus prose fiction, namely the fable and the utopia.

[33] Hopkinson, p. 40.

3

During the thirties, at the same time that he was trying to write novels, George Orwell also wrote his three autobiographical volumes: *Down and Out in Paris and London*, *The Road to Wigan Pier* and *Homage to Catalonia*. Like the novels these books have as their underlying theme the quest for an authentic sense of selfhood. The crucial defect of the novels is, as we have seen, the lack of felt experience in them, a flaw which is directly involved with their derivativeness. What gives the autobiographies far greater distinction and interest is that in them Orwell gradually frees himself from inherited categories and thereby comes to perceive and to record experience freshly, vividly and in his own terms.

At first sight these books may appear to be just reportage of the kind that was so much in vogue during the thirties. Indeed it is very likely that in great part they were intended as such. For Orwell did not find it easy to write with confidence about himself. There are many occasions where he strikes us as a very shy and reticent autobiographer. Nevertheless, whatever his conscious purposes may have been, Orwell is very much present in these books and this presence rather than the reporting is what gives them their liveliness and their continuing interest. We can go further and particularise this Orwellian presence by applying to the three books a definition of autobiography offered by Roy Pascal in his recent study of the subject. For they are "not only an account of things done or known, an exposition of a personality, but a search for the true self and a means to come to terms with it."[34] One unmistakable feature of these autobio-

[34] Roy Pascal, *Design and Truth in Autobiography* (Cambridge, Mass., 1960), p. 39.

graphies and the one which most immediately establishes them as a work of human rather than merely documentary significance is Orwell's implicit confession of the paucity, the unreality even, of his experience. This particular sense of deprivation is the chief premise, the thematic starting point, of all the books. Orwell was a man oppressed by a certain emotional vacuousness both within himself and in his relations with the world about him. And his personal history as he has recorded it is an unceasing quest for experience sufficiently intense to make for a convincing validation of the self. This explains the important fact that the experiences which these three volumes report were ones which Orwell deliberately and determinedly and urgently sought out; they were all very much premeditated excursions into experience. Furthermore, they were social as well as, so to speak, geographical excursions. For although the actual locations, Paris, the depressed North of England and Civil War Spain, are of considerable significance, the main point to be noted is that these journeys were undertaken in order to escape from the seeming unreality of English middle-class life into the less debilitatingly ambiguous world of the poor and the oppressed. Orwell, we may say, was in search of what Hofmannsthal once called "un contact fécond avec les hommes et les choses", the sort of rich direct contact that could provide him with the feeling of being fully alive, fully realised as a human being. As we consider the individual volumes, we shall see that this issue is at the heart of each of them.

The first and least mature of the autobiographies, *Down and Out in Paris and London,* was published in 1933. This book comprises two distinct parts. The first deals with Orwell's time in Paris in the late twenties; it describes his experience of poverty and near starvation there and his subsequent jobs as a *plongeur* or scullion first in the kitchens of a very large hotel and then in a fashionable and "atmospheric" restaurant. The second part of the book treats of his continuing poverty upon his return to England and his experiences living among down and outs and tramps in and around London.

Orwell's emigration to Paris was his first act in following his own bent. The three most formative experiences of his earlier life, his prep school, Eton and then his career as a policeman in Burma, were all events which happened before he was sufficiently adult to think and to decide for himself. The reasons why Paris should be the object of Orwell's first free essay in experience are not far to seek. Given his aspirations to be a writer and his strong admiration for Zola and especially for symbolist writers such as Baudelaire and Proust, it follows that he should wish to know at first hand the city which appeared to him to be the origin and still the home of all that was important in modern literature. The somewhat romanticised idea of the Paris of the artists which the young Orwell appears to have cherished in his intellectual solitude in Burma finds expression in a passage in *Burmese Days*. The idea is grossly caricatured; but this does not necessarily deny its attraction for Orwell at one stage of his life. The speaker is Flory who, as we have already remarked, may be seen as the surrogate of Orwell himself as a young man. He is speaking to Elizabeth Lackersteen who has just come to Burma from Paris where her mother has been "being an artist":

> "Paris! Have you really lived in Paris? . . . I've never seen it. But, good Lord, how I've imagined it! Paris—it's all a kind of jumble of pictures in my mind; cafés and boulevards and artists' studios and Villon and Baudelaire and Maupassant all mixed up together. You don't know how the names of those European towns sound to us, out here. And did you really live in Paris? Sitting in cafés with foreign art students, drinking white wine and talking about Marcel Proust?"

The pathetically conventional sentimentality of this idea is something which Orwell could obviously see through (clearly, he is very determined to let us know that he can see through it) at the time that he wrote this novel. Certainly, by then, he had already spent some time in Paris and inevitably had found it different from his expectations. For at that time Paris was not in one of those stages of literary ferment important to Anglo-Saxons. All vestiges of the nineties, of the Paris of Zola and Villiers and Mallarmé and Yeats and Wilde, linger though they might in Orwell's mind, were gone. The city which he knew was one which could not easily be romanticised by the man of letters. In the essay "Inside the Whale" Orwell described his time there as "a story of bug-ridden rooms in working-mens' hotels, of fights, drinking bouts, cheap brothels, Russian refugees, cadging, swindling and temporary jobs". Throughout the Paris section of the book Orwell stresses heavily and repeatedly the unromantic features of the city as he knew it. "Poverty is what I am writing about," he announces early on and then follow detailed accounts of what it is like to live in Paris without money, of the several dealings which Orwell and his friend Boris had with the state pawn shops, of the sordid details of extreme hunger and near starvation, of the filthiness of hotel kitchens and the prostrating hard work of a scullion.

But despite his tendency to debunk the Paris of romance, Orwell clearly remained enthralled by the idea of it which he had gained from books. In Paris there are two Orwells, one who seeks to prevent himself from being "taken in" and another who cannot hide his preoccupation that Paris must provide him with commemorable experience. If Orwell often dwells upon the mundane and the squalid, he also at times insists on making Paris conform to his idea of what it should be and on seeing it through the eyes of earlier writers. The opening paragraphs of the book, for instance, in which Orwell sets out in impression-istic and often verbless sentences "to convey something of the spirit of the Rue de Coq d'Or", "the atmosphere of the street", could be indebted to any one of a host of writers about Paris from Hemingway to Elliot Paul. And throughout the book there are numerous literary echoes. Murger's *Vie de Bohème* appears to have coloured many of the anecdotes as well as the pictures of working-class merrymaking. The story of Roucolle the miser is straight Balzac, and Boris, the most important character in this first half of the book, is very much of the world of *Ninotchka* and Jacques Deval's *Tovaritch*. Most important of all, we have, in Charlie, Orwell's obviously fascinated account of a latterday and somewhat vulgarised Axel. There is nothing in Orwell's autobiographies which more clearly reveals his early infatuation with the French nineties, the decadence, the period that saw the birth of *le symbolisme* than the many descriptions of Charlie, his life and loves and table talk.

Charlie is a young man living in the same quarter of Paris as Orwell. Like Axel, Charlie is absolutely sure about what was the happiest day of his life and he recalls it at some length. He had gone, we are told, to a brothel which was fitted out exclusively in red. "Red carpet on the floor, red paper on the walls, red plush on the chairs, even the ceiling red; red everywhere red, burning into the eyes. It was a heavy stifling red, as though the light were shining through bowls of blood." Even the child prostitute who receives Charlie is dressed in red. (This is of course, a situation which calls to mind a very famous episode in decadent literature, the dinner party given by des Esseintes in *A Rebours*, though there the colour fetishism settled upon a completely black decor, even to the point, it may be remembered, of employing naked negresses to serve as waitresses.) Charlie now proceeds to describe how he made love to the little girl in red. His words might have come straight from the pages of Villiers.

> You, *messieurs et dames*, you who have not cultivated the finer sensibilities of love, for you such pleasure is almost beyond conception. And I too, now that my youth is gone—ah, youth—shall never again see life so beautiful as that. It is finished.
>
> Ah yes, it is gone—gone forever. Ah the poverty, the shortness, the disappointment of human joy! For in reality—*car en réalité*, what is the duration of the supreme moment of love? It is nothing, an instant, a second perhaps. A second of ecstasy, and after that—dust, ashes, nothingness.
>
> And so, just for one instant, I captured the supreme happiness, the highest and most refined emotion to which human beings can attain. And in the same moment it was finished, and I was left—to what? All my savagery, my passion were scattered like the petals of a rose.

There is absolutely nothing in the context to suggest that Orwell intended this long string of *fin de siècle* clichés as parody. The reason that he offers for presenting Charlie is "just to show what diverse characters could be found flourishing in the Coq d'Or quarter." And I think we can only conclude that at this stage of his life Orwell was sufficiently naïve and gullible to be impressed by this sort of figure. Charlie is offered to us straightforwardly as an object of fascination and also, we may suspect, as a proof of the breadth of Orwell's own worldliness and experience.

He is also there as one of Orwell's several devices for shocking his middle-class reader. Given the year in which the book was published, Charlie and his wickedness are a pathetically superannuated set of weapons for such a purpose. So also is the provocative contrast between Paris and London which is implied in the title of the book and developed in its pages. This itself derives from a tradition in English writing which flourished particularly strongly in the nineties and was perpetuated in the twentieth century by, among others, Chesterton, Belloc and some of the Bloomsbury writers. It is from this tradition of literary francophilia that Orwell, in the Paris section of his book, borrows much of his outlook.[35] He takes great pleasure in the thought of himself as an old Paris hand ("You can live on a shilling a day in Paris if you know how") and in making comparisons unfavourable to England. A paragraph describing the jollities at the *bistro* which Orwell frequented ends with the comment, "I wish one could find a pub in London a quarter as cheery." Again, his initial impression of London upon his return from Paris is that "It was queer after Paris; everything was so much cleaner and quieter and drearier. One missed the scream of the trams, and the noisy, festering life of the back streets, and the armed men clattering through the squares." Such distinctions recur throughout the book, and often upon the slightest of pretexts. "I had been in London innumerable times, and yet until that day I had never noticed one of the worst things about London—the fact that it costs money even to sit down. In Paris, if you had no money and could not find a public bench, you could sit on the pavement." And of Bozo, whom of all the tramps he encountered in England Orwell admired most, we are told with some suggestion of approval that "France suited him better than England (he despised the English). . . ."

This particular method of trying to *épater le bourgeois* loses effectiveness precisely because it employs thereto a set of literary

[35] An interesting history of the type of writing to which the first half of *Down and Out in Paris and London* belongs may be found in Christophe Campos, *The View of France, from Arnold to Bloomsbury* (London, 1965).

devices that are such a familiar feature in English middle-class writing. And it is not only these particular literary mannerisms that make us conscious of Orwell's middle-class origins and background. The fact of Orwell the old Etonian is brought home to us time and time again and overwhelmingly by the nature of the writing. (There is, for instance, the moment when Orwell discovers that in a certain casual ward he must sleep on the floor and immediately exclaims, "But I say, damn it, where are the beds?" There is also the recurrent use of the word "beastly" and here and there the revealing simile: "And yet it was excellent tea, as different from coffee shop tea as good Bordeaux is from the muck called colonial claret.") Nevertheless, even though Orwell is still closely bound to his native class in his way with the language and thus in his manner of feeling and responding, it is also true that the central theme of this book is his endeavour—his undeniable need—to dissociate himself from this self-same class. This theme is developed most convincingly and compellingly not in the Paris section of the book, which reveals the same sort of susceptibility to the prevailing literary orthodoxy that is to be found in the novels, but rather in those sections proposed by the words "down and out". This is the part of the book that strikes us as the most deeply felt and as the most authentically Orwellian. It represents Orwell's first essay in making a new way of life and also, in consequence, a new way with the language. It relates the beginning of that moral endeavour which continues as the major topic of all the subsequent autobiographical documents. As a literary sightseer in Paris Orwell often strikes us as gawkily ingenuous, but as a refugee from his native class, as an explorer into the social underworld of his time, he deals with what are to him urgent realities.

The experience of being down and out is broached awkwardly and with considerable uncertainty. For Orwell poverty is not only a financial state, a stratum of society or a social evil, but also a source of personal terror. It is, in his own words, "the thing you knew would happen to you sooner or later". The use of the second person here seems to carry some suggestion of a desire to implicate the reader in this same fear and doom. And elsewhere in the book we find other examples of a similar chattiness implying that author and reader share the same assumptions. But on other occasions Orwell loses this confidence. His tone and attitude change radically; he tries to hector and to shock the reader with his knowledge of poverty and all its sordid details, as if trying to force him out of his complacency and indifference to it. This uneasiness seems to derive from Orwell's doubt as to the acceptability of caste and particularly the experience of loss of caste as subjects for discussion. The first effect of Orwell's estrangement from middle-class life is a tonal uncertainty in his style, an uncertainty about his relationship with his middle-class reader.

"O scathful harm, condition of poverte!" The Chaucerian epigraph to *Down and Out in Paris and London* could stand equally appropriately before many of Orwell's subsequent writings. For this before all else is the subject that preoccupies him. It figures as a perpetually looming sanction over all who live in a hierarchical society and who hold any rank, position or status within that society. It signifies a permanent threat of humiliation, a profound displacement in relationships with others: "Dressed in a tramp's clothes it is very difficult, at any rate for the first day, not to feel that you are genuinely degraded." It is the image which for Orwell invokes a whole nexus of deformed feeling both in the self and in others. Later on in his career Orwell will become confident enough to approach and to discuss frankly this malady of middle-class life. But in this first book he is clearly inhibited by his sense of offending against social and literary good form in mentioning what it is the convention to ignore. Here, at the outset of his career, he is still sufficiently the prisoner of his class that he feels it necessary to some extent to tone down, even to falsify, the true nature of his experience and awareness. Some account of the discrepancies in Orwell's narrative will help to reveal this fundamental contradiction in his mind, a contradiction which in changing form recurs throughout the autobiographies and which it was his life's work to resolve.

From what we are told in *Down and Out in Paris and London* it would seem that Orwell became a down-and-out purely as a result of a sequence of circumstances over which he had no control. His troubles in Paris begin, it is suggested, when the greater part of his money is stolen one night from his hotel room. This brings him to what he terms "the suburbs, as it were, of poverty", a situation in which, predictably, he still struggles "to keep up appearances". Soon after, however, the English lessons which he gives and which we assume are his only source of income come to an abrupt end. He is now completely impoverished and is forced to pawn most of his clothes. In an effort to get help in finding a job he seeks out an old acquaintance, Boris, a White Russian officer turned waiter. But Boris is in even more desperate straits than Orwell himself. The Russian seeks help from his creditors, but without avail, and so Orwell and Boris together experience a lengthy period of poverty and extreme hunger. Eventually, however, Boris finds employment at the Hotel X, where he also manages to get Orwell a job as a scullion. Here and later in the kitchens of the Auberge de Jehan Cottard Orwell experiences the sort of intense hard work that makes him "neurasthenic with fatigue". Since he does not feel "equal to going on with a seventeen hour day", he writes to his friend B in London to ask if he can find him a job in England. B replies that there is a job available looking after a congenital imbecile. Orwell immediately accepts it. On his return to London, however, he finds that his future employers together with the imbecile have gone abroad and that there will be a three month delay before he can take up his strange new employment. With only nineteen shillings and sixpence in his pocket, Orwell finds himself once again compelled to live "in some hole and corner way". He exchanges his clothes for those of a tramp and lodges in a succession of ever cheaper and dirtier lodging-houses. Finally he has recourse to the casual wards, the "spikes", of the London area; and we are given accounts of those at Romton, Edbury, Crowley, and Lower Binfield. Orwell also finds a new "mate" in Paddy, a tramp whom he meets in the first casual ward that he visits. And through Paddy he is brought into contact with numerous "characters" in the begging and tramping community. With the help of a loan of two pounds from B, Orwell is able to survive until it is time for his job to begin. And here the book ends.

Reading through Orwell's account of these adventures, one cannot but note some implausible elements in it.[36] For instance, when speaking of his decision to go and seek out Boris, Orwell

[36] John Wain has also commented upon what he calls "the

remarks with a ponderous irony calculated to emphasise the extremity of the situation that "It was a great relief to remember that I had after all one influential friend to fall back on." But the reader recalls that in the preceding chapter Orwell had mentioned at least one "prosperous friend" in Paris and must wonder if the road to Boris and to poverty was really the only one open to Orwell at that time. It also appears improbable that it was absolutely necessary for Orwell to go down and out among the tramps of London. Surely with the firm prospect of a job it would have been possible and proper for him to borrow enough from B to live "respectably" during the months before his employment was due to begin. The suspicions we may come to have about this whole episode are confirmed by Orwell's restatement of it in *The Road to Wigan Pier*, a book which differs from its predecessor above all by virtue of the greater frankness and confidence with which it is written. Speaking there of this earlier book, Orwell first of all concedes that *"nearly all* the incidents described there actually happened, though they have been rearranged." (Italics mine.) However, in the light of the new version which he now gives of his entry into poverty in London, this would appear to be very much an understatement. For he now reports that his joining the down-and-outs was a deliberate decision on his part. His experience as a police officer in Burma, he tells us, had created in him a deep guilt about belonging to the ruling class: "What I profoundly wanted at that time, was to find some way of getting out of the respectable world altogether." There follows a sentence which tells us much about Orwell, even something of the reasons for his adoption of a pseudonym: "I meditated upon it a great deal, I even planned parts of it in detail; how one could sell everything, give everything away, change one's name and start out with no money and nothing but the clothes one stood up in." And in the event, his excursion into poverty was carefully pre-arranged. "One evening," he tells us, *"having made ready at a friend's house*, I set out and wandered eastward till I landed up at a common lodging-house in Limehouse Causeway. It was

curiously evasive streak" in this portion of *Down and Out in Paris and London*; see John Wain, "George Orwell II" in *Essays in Literature and Ideas* (London, 1963), pp. 201, 202.

a dark, dirty-looking place. I knew it was a common lodging-house by the sign 'Good Beds for Single Men' in the window. Heavens how I had to screw up my courage before I went in." (Italics mine.)

So much then for the story of the congenital idiot. Quite obviously Orwell's experience of poverty occurred not as a result of circumstances, but rather in answer to the demands of his own psychological condition. It is equally clear that Orwell was unable at this time to be frank about this condition, and felt obliged to disguise it as a set of uncourted picaresque adventures calculated to win the reader's tolerance by amusing and entertaining him. The extent of Orwell's authorial difficulties with the whole situation can be gauged by the extreme fatuousness of the device of the congenital idiot. In the later autobiographies this embarrassment disappears. There he will be able to identify his deep impulse to know the underworld of the poor not as a ludicrous or morbid piece of eccentricity, but rather as one of his several impulses to extend his awareness and to find liberation from the constricting illusions of middle-class life. It is an impulse that will stay with Orwell throughout his life. The occasion described above was not the only one upon which Orwell was to go a to friend's house in order to don his disguise. Sir Richard Rees has described another:

> He came to my house one day and asked if he might change his clothes. Having left his respectable suit in the bedroom, he went off again dressed more or less in rags. He wanted, he said, to know about prison from the inside and he hoped that if he were picked up drunk and disorderly in the East End he might manage to achieve this. Next day he appeared very crestfallen. He had duly got drunk and been taken to a police station. But once there he had received a fatherly talk, spent the night in a cell and been let out next morning with a cup of tea and some good advice.[37]

This brings out very clearly the comic aspect of Orwell's quest, the comedy of the cloth-capped Quixote. It is the sort of comedy endemic to any situation in which there is anxiety to know things "from the inside". But I have cited the incident chiefly because it illustrates Orwell's perseverance in his quest. In some

[37] Rees, p. 136.

sense all the autobiographical volumes and a great number of the essays are similar accounts of an unceasing effort to exorcise delusions by gaining access to the reality, however harsh it may be, that underlies them.

At this point I should say that it is not to my purpose to make any contrast between Orwell's account of himself and the accounts set down by friends and other witnesses which might be supposed to be more "objective". For purposes of emphasis I have felt free to cite the above incident since it is but a corroboration of a feature of Orwell's behaviour which he himself described in *The Road to Wigan Pier*. But this is the only way in which I shall use such secondary sources. As is well known, Orwell was anxious that no biography of him should ever be written. John Atkins informs us that when he died he left a request to this effect and adds that "He used to say that truthful biography was impossible because every life viewed from the inside would be a series of defeats too disgraceful and humiliating to contemplate."[38] This wish for privacy is something which I have no desire to infringe. My concern is in no way with speculation or gossip, but rather, and exclusively, with the literary qualities of the histories of his experience which Orwell himself saw fit to write down and publish. To be sure there is in these writings a clear discrepancy between what we may term the actual self and the created self. But this discrepancy registered as it is in the words that make up the autobiography is a legitimate object for literary scrutiny. Indeed it is this very discrepancy which particularly engages us. For Orwell's story is essentially one of a continuing struggle to escape from the concept of self with which he was endowed by birth and background. It is the story of an attempted escape from an inherited set of attitudes, responses and feelings which made for pain, for vital impoverishment and for a sense of life as something unreal and the story of an effort to renew and to recreate the self in such a way as to make for more abundant life.

In this regard the fact that Orwell chose to use a pseudonym is of considerable importance. For it seems very likely that Eric Blair was associated with the original and unregenerate self and that the decision to assume another name constituted one

[38] Atkins, p. 31.

of the first steps towards self-renewal. Laurence Brander has told us of what is perhaps the most obvious and certainly the most often mentioned reason for Orwell's use of the pseudonym: "It is said that he disliked his own name because it showed that he was a Scot; and that he disliked Scotland because it was associated with the deer-forests he heard about from rich boys at his prep school, and was therefore a wealthy man's playground."[39] But T. R. Fyvel has restated this in such a way as to suggest the deeper and less easily defined forces at work: "Names are highly symbolical things and, as he knew, his own change of *nom de guerre* surely also represented a deliberate act to cut loose from the past, from his childhood, from certain unresolved conflicts which he could never quite shake off."[40] Furthermore his name never ceased to be a matter of serious importance to him. Atkins tells us, for instance, that "Towards the end of his life he was planning to change his name by deed poll", an action which suggests the final sloughing off of the older self and the establishment of the other as the true and real one, not only in his own eyes but in those of his fellows. Atkins also tells us that Orwell was "impressed by the reverence which primitive people feel for their names".[41] And this together with other occasional references among the biographical critics to mystical tendencies in Orwell[42] (Brander, for example, suggests that the search for the good life through the conscious acceptance of poverty "is an idea which Orwell may very well have picked up in the East".[43]) would corroborate a fact about Orwell's career which can be detected in his writings themselves. It is simply this: his deepest concern was with the remaking of the self. And though because

[39] Brander, p. 2.
[40] T. R. Fyvel, "A Writer's Life." *World Review*, June, 1950.
[41] Atkins, p. 50.
[42] Despite the way he will pooh-pooh the occult later on in life (in the essay on Yeats, for instance), there is nevertheless some suggestion that he took the idea of witchcraft seriously. Sir Richard Rees relates that when he enquired of Orwell concerning the pseudonym, "he told me that it gave him an unpleasant feeling to see his real name in print because 'how can you be sure your enemy won't take it out and work some black magic on it?'" Sir Richard adds that "you could not always be certain if he was serious or not."
[43] Brander, p. 16.

of a certain reticence and reserve he broaches this primarily in social and political terms, we neglect the most important aspect of his autobiography if we acquiesce in the widespread tendency to categorise him exclusively as a writer on social and political issues.

But here I find myself unduly ahead of the stage of discussion we had reached and must return to the consideration of Orwell's first recorded encounter with poverty, in Paris. The effect of this self-imposed experience was twofold. First, the direct confrontation of horror brings "a feeling of relief, almost of pleasure, at knowing yourself at long last genuinely down and out". The long harboured and nagging fear has been resolutely embraced and is now to a certain extent overcome. "You have talked so often of going to the dogs—and well, here are the dogs, and you have reached them, and you can stand it. It takes off a lot of anxiety." And secondly, this new knowledge gives him an added confidence in his efforts to shock, belabour and assault those of his fellow bourgeois whose complacent acquiescence in an inhumanly hierarchical order permits the horror to exist. Occasionally there is an element of somewhat malicious comedy in Orwell's determined efforts to force his reader to contemplate the foul realities which it is the purpose of the façade of bourgeois conventions to hide. He treats us, for instance, to a long comparison between the hotel dining-room where the customers sit "in all their splendour—spotless tablecloths, bowls of flowers, mirrors and gilt cornices and painted cherubim . . .", and the "disgusting filth" of the kitchens where the waiters sit around "showing their sweaty armpits . . . sticking their thumbs into the cream pots" and frequently washing their faces in the water in which the crockery was rinsing. And a little later, as if to turn the screw even tighter, Orwell tells of a waiter dipping his fingers into the gravy, "his nasty, greasy fingers which he is forever running through his brilliantined hair". This whole disquisition on hotel cooking concludes with the unpleasant dictum: "Roughly speaking, the more one pays for food, the more sweat and spittle one is obliged to eat with it."

But this sort of humour is not the most characteristic feature of Orwell's assault upon the reader's sensibility. He is usually more direct in his desire to horrify. Challengingly and accusingly he parades a whole series of squalid, sordid details from the lower depths. He dwells on foul smells, dirty underwear, reeking bed linen, the "greasy little cloths known as toe-rags that tramps wear", chamber pots, the filthy water in the public washtubs in the casual wards and above all, and most insistently, upon "bugs", the image which before all others in the England of that time suggested a default in cleanliness, godliness, propriety and respectability. If this insistence upon the unpleasant suggested merely a desire on Orwell's part to be wantonly offensive it could not interest us. But interest it does, and this because we sense that he is trying to compel attention to aspects of reality from which it is customary to turn aside. It is the painful, awkward sincerity of a man trying a bit desperately to convey his horror at a social order which has within it such discrepancies that one extreme can be for the other an unreal and frightening world. And above all it derives from Orwell's intense, even obsessive, revulsion from his own native class which he believes requires this foul underside of life as part of its own definition.

In the final paragraphs of *The Road to Wigan Pier* Orwell will call for the breakdown of these divisions between men and indeed for a political alliance between the middle class and the underprivileged. But in *Down and Out in Paris and London* the call for social justice is less central. It is just one part of Orwell's expression of exasperation at the quality of social life. The policies which he sketches for the improvement of the lot of *plongeurs* and tramps are merely one aspect of his fear of the physical, social and psychological nastiness that derives from a social ordering in which one group is ignorant and ultimately both fearful and contemptuous of another group. Throughout the autobiographies the reportage and the social prescriptions are but different surface manifestations of the same fundamental desire, the desire for a revision of the assumptions upon which people relate to each other. A historian of English working-class experience has recently remarked that "The strength of distinctions of class and status in twentieth-century England is in part a consequence of the lack, in the twentieth-century labour movement, of Jacobin virtues."[44] For Orwell of course

[44] E. P. Thompson, *The Making of the English Working Class* (London, 1964), p. 183.

this lack was more painfully conspicuous in his own middle class, but there is no phrase that better suggests the qualities which he saw as deficient in the life of his time and which he sought to infuse into it than "the Jacobin virtues". As we read through the autobiographies we are increasingly aware of a desire on Orwell's part to approach those whom he meets (and his reader too, for that matter) on the basis not so much of equality (the connotations of that word are now too sterile for what I intend) as of *égalité*. In one of his essays Orwell actually identifies what is valuable for him in working-class people in terms of the English Jacobin tradition and remarks upon "the moral code they derive from the Protestant centuries and the French Revolution".[45] And throughout his writings we find an urgent and fierce determination to discard all the niceties of status, condescension and deference and to establish the principles of self-respect and respect for others as the premises for human dealings.

This in part explains an element common to all three autobiographies, namely Orwell's desire to fraternise and to be identified with those who, being at the base of the class order, have no commitment to the system of attitudes and responses which it enjoins. Orwell's chief motive for going down and out was, as he has told us, a desire to get rid of the guilt he had incurred in Burma by undergoing the same experiences as those whom he regarded as the European equivalents of those he had oppressed. But it is clear that he was also in search of a type and a quality of human relationship which middle-class life precluded. In *Down and Out in Paris and London* the reader is often surprised by the sudden and emphatic use of the first person plural to assert Orwell's membership in the lower orders. Forced by a London charitable organisation to attend a church service in return for some tea, the tramps whom Orwell is with proceed to take their revenge. "It was not long before we were making far more noise than the minister. . . . We had set ourselves to guy the service and there was no stopping us." "What could a few women and old men do against a hundred hostile tramps? They were afraid of us and we were frankly bullying them. It was our revenge upon

[45] George Orwell, "Fascism and Democracy", *The Betrayal of the Left*, ed. Victor Gollancz (London, 1941), p. 215.

them for having humiliated us by feeding us." A similarly self-conscious proclamation of community is contained in a passage in which Orwell is trying to suggest how intense hard work can make people indifferent to everything except the work itself, food and sleep. A murder is committed beneath Orwell's window in the middle of the night. But neither he nor the Parisian working people of the neighbourhood have sufficient energy or interest to pay much attention; "we just made sure that the man was done for, and went straight back to bed. . . . We were working people and where was the sense of wasting sleep over a murder?"

In this last sentence we may detect two of Orwell's characteristically offensive-defensive challenges to the reader. There is the justification of what might be taken for dereliction of civic duty and there is Orwell's parade of association with a community. But here as in so many other passages in the book there is an element of excessive protestation that gives the game away. Nevertheless, even if it is obvious that Orwell is not, nor cannot be, of the submerged classes, and if there is something slightly ridiculous about his pretending that he is, it is equally obvious that this sort of affiliation is a profound psychic necessity for him. The working class is in fact his myth of the good life. And his autobiography claims our interest not so much for what it can tell us about the poor, the underprivileged and the oppressed but for what it reveals about the state of the middle-class mind at a time when it was failing in dynamic and in confidence. Though there are times, even late in his career, when references to "the common people" herald a lapse into a romanticising that derives from the myth rather than from experience, this is not to say that we should dismiss completely the accounts of working-class life which Orwell offers us. One of the most interesting facts about his career is that, alone among modern writers of any repute, he sought continually to validate his personal myth by exploration into the external world. And we can, to a considerable extent, see Orwell's progress as an experiential refinement of his understanding of the working class.

This begins as early as *Down and Out in Paris and London* with Orwell's realisation that the common people as individuals are not necessarily exemplars of those qualities of warmth, directness, neighbourliness, accessibility and *égalité* which as a group they signify in Orwell's imagination. Working in the hotel kitchen in Paris, Orwell comes quickly to perceive "the elaborate caste system existing in a hotel". And what engages him most deeply are not the gradations of prestige represented by the various sorts of jobs (though he does describe them at some length), but rather the distinction between two attitudes to life signified by the words "workman" and "snob". Waiters, we are told, have "the mentality, not of a working man, but of a snob": "They are snobs and they find the servile nature of their work rather congenial." Such indifference to the principle (very much the Jacobin principle) of self-respect is something which Orwell finds repellent. The very phrases and vocabulary of the following sentence, in which Orwell describes the waiter's job, convey the strong animus: "He lives perpetually in sight of rich people, stands at their tables, listens to their conversations, sucks up to them with smiles and discreet little jokes." In the actual context the contempt is sharpened by the contrast between the waiters and the cooks. For the cooks, in Orwell's view, are "the most workmanlike class and the least servile": "The cook does not look upon himself as a servant but as a skilled workman." He has a sense of his function and his value which removes him from the system of condescension and servility which for Orwell is the chief cause of the horror underlying both the psyche and the society of the time. In England, among the tramps, Orwell's realisation that "the poor" comprehend the abject and the obsequious as well as the self-respecting is developed further. In his attitude to Paddy, for instance, who is introduced as Orwell's mate and also as a "typical" tramp, there is a criticism far more biting than that directed towards the Paris waiters. Paddy is seen as "essentially abject", as having "the regular character of a tramp, abject, envious, a jackal's character". It is only in the final paragraph of the chapter devoted to the presentation of Paddy that Orwell bethinks himself and hastily commends his mate for his loyalty and generosity and asserts that "It was malnutrition and not any native vice that had destroyed his manhood." But this sudden compassion and admiration seems merely formal. It is not as sincerely felt as the disgust and the contempt that are registered in the earlier phrases. And certainly this whole chapter does much to invalidate the innocent egalitarianism of Orwell which we have encountered earlier in the book—for instance, in his intense denial of the proposition that "there is some mysterious fundamental difference between rich and poor."

But if Orwell's myth is called in question by experience, it is also at the same time confirmed by it. There are cooks as well as waiters, and in England there is not only Paddy, there is also Bozo. Bozo is by far the most important character in the book. He is a "screever", a pavement artist whom Orwell meets through Paddy and whom he comes to regard as "a very exceptional man". For though Bozo has a very badly deformed leg and though there was "clearly no future for him but beggary and death in the workhouse", he is the embodiment of all those qualities so important to Orwell. He is contemptuous of the relationship between the patronised and the patronising and refuses to accept help from the religious charities and to "sing hymns for buns". Also there is in him the sort of militancy which Orwell seems to find exciting; "He was the enemy of society, and quite ready to take to crime if he saw a good opportunity." But what impresses Orwell most of all is Bozo's interest in literary and intellectual matters and his determination not to be reduced to a single-minded concern for "tea and two slices". Bozo, it turns out, "had read some of Zola's novels, all Shakespeare's plays, *Gulliver's Travels,* and a number of essays". He is also an amateur astronomer and has received acknowledgement from the Astronomer Royal for his reports on meteors. Bozo, in fact, is a living and heroic testimony to a quality of life and culture which may be sustained in the face of a hostile material environment and in opposition to the established pattern of human and social relationships. For like Orwell himself, he despises the English middle class: "You'll never get a drop off real toffs. It's shabby sort of blokes you get most off, and foreigners." And like Orwell he also despises the readiness of someone like Paddy to accept humiliation: "Look at Paddy —a tea-swilling old moocher, only fit to scrounge for fag ends. That's the way most of them go. I despise them. But you don't *need* to get like that . . . You just got to say to yourself, 'I'm a free man in *here*,'—he tapped his forehead—'and you're all right.'"

Orwell's acquaintance with Bozo is the most important experience described in the book. It not only helps to confirm Orwell's myth about those who live below and beyond the middle class, it also affords him new possibilities of tone and outlook. In his progress towards a new mode of selfhood Orwell assimilates much from Bozo. One measure of the strength of the impression that Bozo makes is that certain of his characteristics stay with Orwell and reappear years later in his writings. Bozo's particular gesture of intellectual freedom, for instance, is something which will be taken over by Winston Smith. And his embittered atheism, his "pleasure in thinking human affairs would never improve", is also the attitude of Benjamin, the moralist of *Animal Farm*. The influence is clear enough. But possibly because of his own uncertainties about himself, Orwell is awkward when he attempts to give some account of what this friendship meant to him. The abrupt and nervously concessive sentence that is tacked on to the end of one of the paragraphs describing Bozo—"One could not help admiring him,"— is clearly inadequate, pathetically inadequate, to the quality of the friendship which actually existed. Even the straightforward descriptions of Bozo and of his particular moral achievement sometimes come perilously close to rank sentimentality, the sentimentality which is likely to attach to any urgent demand that we admire a courageous underdog. ("He might be ragged and cold, or even starving, but so long as he could read, think and watch for meteors, he was, as he said, free in his own mind.") Only when Orwell presents the friendship in terms of specific incidents and conversation is he able to convey the authentic particularities of the relationship. At one point, for example, Bozo tells Orwell of a cremation which he had witnessed when a soldier in India:

> "They put the old chap on the fire, and the next moment, I almost jumped out of my skin, because he'd started kicking. It was only his muscles contracting in the heat—still, it gave me a turn. Well, he wriggled about for a bit like a kipper on hot coals, and then his belly blew up and went off with a bang you could have heard fifty yards away. It fair put me off cremation."

This anecdote could well be one of Orwell's own horror stories. (One is reminded, for instance, of the grim comedy in the description of the man trampled to death by the elephant in the essay "Shooting an Elephant".) And one wonders whether Orwell's pleasure in the humour of the horrible derived from, or was merely reinforced by, his acquaintance with Bozo. But at all events, just from the evidence of this incident alone, we can sense the community of feeling between them. Both know of horror in life, both insist on facing it directly and both respond to it with the homely understatement that re-establishes the good cheer that is necessary for living. Bozo, remarks Orwell admiringly, "had faced his position, and made a philosophy for himself." And it is because Bozo, albeit in somewhat different terms, has dealt with the same fundamental problems with which Orwell himself must deal, the problems of creating the self and of resisting the deadening effect of prevalent social attitudes, that he marks one of the most important stages in Orwell's career.

Down and Out in Paris and London has for its essential themes Orwell's abandonment of his half-hearted attempt to pose as the fashionable *littérateur* and his first ventures in exorcising that paralysing fear of a radical social displacement which he feels to be an inherent, indeed a characterising, feature of the psychology of his class. The book leads us to conclude that this endeavour was to some extent successful, though it is perhaps inappropriate in this regard to speak of conclusion. For *Down and Out in Paris and London* leaves us above all with the impression of inconclusiveness, of being a work in progress, a first chapter even. Orwell actually ends the book in a mood of dissatisfaction. The penultimate paragraph conveys both a strong sense of separation from the free and colourful poor and an urgent, even obsessive, desire to understand them more deeply. "Some day I want to explore that world more thoroughly. I should like to know people like Mario and Paddy and Bill the moocher, not from casual encounters but intimately; I should like to understand what really goes on in the souls of *plongeurs* and tramps and embankment sleepers."

Orwell's attempt to achieve this renewal of contact with the social underworld is the subject of his second book of autobiography, *The Road to Wigan Pier*, which was published in 1937.

Though here the people who engage his attention are significantly different from those in the first. Orwell travelled to the North of England, he tells us, "partly because I wanted to see what mass unemployment is like at its worst, partly in order to see the most typical section of the English working class at close quarters." However it is obvious from the pages of *The Road to Wigan Pier* that the northern working people were far less ready to permit casual recruitment than the down-and-outs of Paris and London had been. This second work of autobiography differs greatly from its predecessor in mood and temper. But the root difference, the determining difference, is that in *The Road to Wigan Pier* there is absolutely no evidence of memorable contact with any member of the social group which Orwell had come expressly to seek out and to know. The only working men that Orwell is able to name and to describe for us are those whom he meets while staying at the Brookers' shabby lodging-house in Lancashire. And these for the most part excite in him little interest or admiration; they are characterised and dismissed very briefly. "The Scotch miner was a bore when you got to know him." Joe is just a quickly sketched Dickensian caricature; "He often said to me, 'Matrimonial chains is a big item', evidently feeling this to be a very subtle and portentous remark." And as for the Brookers themselves, they are as repellent as the combination tripe shop and boarding-house they run. If anything, they are for Orwell subhuman, not just because of the terrible physical squalor of their lives but also on account of the way they mouth a few set responses such as "It does seem 'ard, don't it now?" "The most dreadful thing about the Brookers is the way they say the same things over and over again. It gives you the feeling that they are not real people at all, but a kind of ghost forever rehearsing the same futile rigmarole." The only person residing at the Brookers' who is of any interest at all to Orwell is Old Jack, an ex-miner who had worked in the pits for more than fifty years. "He was alert and intelligent, but curiously enough he seemed only to remember his boyhood experiences and to have forgotten all about the modern mining machinery and improvements." Like Bozo, the old man is jealous of his self-respect, and it is for this chiefly that Orwell esteems him. "What I most admired about Old Jack was that he never cadged; he was generally out of tobacco towards the end of the week but he always refused to smoke anyone else's." However, the encounter with the old miner is not a very important experience for Orwell. He is just a fleeting acquaintance, cursorily presented and cursorily admired. And for the rest of the book the working class is present not as individual human beings, but as a series of generalisations and commended attitudes and values. The actual people whom Orwell met on his trip to the North are always referred to in rather vague terms. He speaks easily of "your miner friends" and tells us, "I always had some local friends among the unemployed." And this is as close as we ever get to an understanding of Orwell's actual relationships with working people. There was, it is clear, an unbridgeable distance between him and the people he desired so urgently to know. Nowhere is this distance better suggested than at the end of the first chapter where Orwell describes a young woman whom he glimpses momentarily from a train window. "I had time to see everything about her—her sacking apron, her clumsy clogs, her arms reddened by the cold. She looked up as the train passed, and I was almost near enough to catch her eye. She had a round pale face, the usual exhausted face of the slum girl who is twenty-five and looks forty, thanks to miscarriages and drudgery; and it wore, for the second in which I saw it, the most desolate hopeless expression I have ever seen." Later on Orwell refers to his "pictures of Lancashire", and this phrase conveys very accurately what he gained from his stay there; not experiences, but rather fleeting images and pictures.

The absence of any specific human involvement is not difficult to explain. Orwell's own several observations on "class breaking" in the latter half of the book demonstrate a keenly personal awareness of the problems in such an undertaking. Indeed an important feature of *The Road to Wigan Pier* in terms of Orwell's development is his admission, his assertion even, of the extent to which his life is characterised unalterably by its middle-class circumstances. The toying with disguises and with the possibilities of assimilation into the society of the underprivileged such as we find in *Down and Out in Paris and London* is now abandoned. Accepting the fact of middle-class style as one of the definitions of his nature, Orwell's concern is now chiefly with speculation upon the middle-class condition and upon the painful debilities which for him this condition implies. *The Road to Wigan Pier* differs from both *Down and Out in Paris and London* and *Homage to Catalonia* in that it is primarily an introspective book. The first and third volumes of the autobiography are accounts of important phases in Orwell's life in which he managed to enter into fruitful relationship with the world beyond himself. But the second book is the one in which he looks most steadfastly into himself, traces his emotional and intellectual history, endeavours to define his particular and intense psychological discomfort and considers in personal and social terms ways of restoring emotional integrity. It is a book of reminiscence and self-analysis. Most of all it is an essay in the anatomising of personal feeling, feeling that is registered in the succession of images that dominates the book. And here I am referring not only to the images of working-class life in Lancashire, though these and the complexes of feeling which they involve are an important part of the enterprise, but also to the series of images recovered from his early life, through which Orwell seeks to establish his emotional history. Whatever else it is, autobiography is an attempt to assess the interaction of past and present in a man's life. And *The Road to Wigan Pier* is the first published of Orwell's endeavours to understand present disharmonies within the self in terms of past experience, and also in the light of valuable experiences in the present to judge influential experiences of the past.

Before proceeding to consider the specifics of this essay in emotional history, I must concede that my insistence upon *The Road to Wigan Pier* as a work of introspective autobiography runs somewhat counter to the ostensible and even the declared intentions of the book. Its instigation was, after all, a commission from the Left Book Club for a report on the conditions of the unemployed in the North of England. And to the editors of that series who were the first readers of the book it appeared as above all a political work. Indeed one of the editors, Mr. Victor Gollancz, was sufficiently impressed by Orwell's criticism of modern socialism and socialists to feel it necessary to write some introductory pages refuting Orwell's charges. Certainly there is good reason for regarding the book both as a political tract and as a piece of left-wing sociologising. Nevertheless, to see it exclusively or even primarily in these terms is to make an improper emphasis. Orwell's political criticism and proposals are all deductions from intensely personal experience, and the condition of England as it is presented in this book is much more compelling as a metaphor of Orwell's own emotional state than as an account of a particular phase of social and political life. The sociological reporting also seems to be very much a subsidiary item in the book. The very structuring of *The Road to Wigan Pier* suggests a conscious effort on Orwell's part to subordinate this aspect of the work to more urgent autobiographical concerns.

The book is divided into two halves and the detailed and sometimes statistical accounts of the mining industry, of the life of the unemployed, of their budgeting and dietary problems, of the conditions of the slums and of the problems of slum clearance are all confined to the first half. But this opening section has more to it than a series of rather amateur sociological reports. It is framed and interspersed with essays on Orwell's own private feelings and attitudes. And these serve not only to relieve the tedium of the factual reporting, but also to establish from the outset the very personal perspective of the book and to prepare the way for the straightforward autobiographical writing at the opening of the second half. The complex of feeling which forms the prominent setting for the sociologising can be suggested by a consideration of the first and final chapters of the first half of the book, the chapters, that is to say, which serve it as a frame. There is a very striking contrast between the two. The first conveys Orwell's tensely controlled horror at the squalor of life imaged by the Brookers' lodging-house and its residents; the chapter is dominated by his feeling of "having got down into some subterranean place where people go creeping round and round, just like blackbeetles . . .". The final chapter, however, expresses altogether different feelings about the homes of working people. It concludes with a series of images of "the peculiar easy completeness, the perfect symmetry, as it were, of a working-class interior at its best" and of the "warm, decent, deeply human atmosphere which it is not so easy to find elsewhere". These

67

two opposing attitudes also find expression in the other accounts of personal feeling in the first half of *The Road to Wigan Pier*. For, instance, the coal mine that Orwell tours elicits the same sort of horror that the Brookers' house (another "subterranean place") had done. The mine, Orwell reports, was "like hell, or at any rate like my own mental picture of hell". But if the miners' situation inspires fear and horror, there is yet again a complicating of the response by virtue of the respect, admiration and affection which Orwell comes to feel for them. What in fact underlies the sociology of the first half of the book is Orwell's series of efforts to reformulate two very divergent emotional impulses which exist independently of any specific social situation. For it is clear that the dilemma which preoccupies Orwell's mind while he is ostensibly serving as a reporter for the Left Book Club is precisely the same dilemma he had tried to solve experientially in *Down and Out in Paris and London*. It is a dilemma involving the tension between horror and desire for that real world which for Orwell exists below the illusion-ridden world of the middle-class consciousness. Or, to redefine it in such a way as to downplay its obtrusive social context, we may say that Orwell's situation as it is reiterated in the first half of *The Road to Wigan Pier* is that of the novice in experience seeking to interpret his perplexing journey through those infernal subterranean regions which make for terror, but which also make for liberation and growth.

To recognise the pre-eminence of this theme is to set at a discount Orwell's justification for relating personal history when at the opening of the second half of the book he proceeds to develop a further stage of his autobiography. There he maintains that his main concerns are with socialism and with "the terribly difficult issue of class". And he excuses the "certain amount of autobiography" he is about to write by remarking that "I would not do it if I did not think that I am sufficiently typical of my class, or rather sub-caste, to have a certain symptomatic importance." Clearly these words constitute a very inadequate account of the real point of all that follows. Rather they seem evidence of Orwell's anxiety about presenting private concerns in such a way as to make them intelligible and acceptable in terms of the current nomenclature of the literary culture.

What we see in these words is in fact the same lack of confidence which led Orwell to pose as the nineties *littérateur* and as the facetious picaro in the earlier volume. Only now, in the mid-thirties, the conventions have changed and Orwell feels constrained to present himself as something of a sociological specimen. The pretext of sociological discourse makes for a more poised book than did the pretexts employed in *Down and Out in Paris and London*. Nevertheless it remains just a pretext, a device that is, for establishing the necessary initial entente with the reader. And ulterior to the pretext is a set of concerns whose significance we improperly curtail if we are persuaded to conceive of them solely as matters of social and political analysis.

We observe for instance that Orwell's first essay in reminiscence, his recollection of his very first awareness of class distinctions, entails what is also a keenly personal memory of his exclusion from the rich and vivid experience of childhood. What is formally offered to us as the first stage in the history of a representative social case is quickly endowed with the qualities of some eminently private myth of a lost Eden. Orwell tells us that prior to this crucial moment in his development, his chief heroes had generally been working-class people, because "they always seemed to do such interesting things such as being fishermen and blacksmiths and bricklayers." He goes on to say, "I remember the farm hands on a farm in Cornwall who used to let me ride on the drill when they were sowing turnips and would sometimes catch the ewes and milk them to give me a drink; and the workmen building a new house next door, who let me play with the wet mortar and from whom I first learned the word 'b——'; and the plumber up the road with whose children I used to go out birdnesting." Orwell's estrangement from this sort of experience occurs when he is told that such people are "common" and is forbidden to play with them. Examining this event as an adult he is able to understand his parents' motives, "for middle-class people cannot afford to let their children grow up with vulgar accents." Nevertheless he does not doubt the crippling consequences for his future development of this moment of enforced self-consciousness or of the severance from what he now conceives as the natural and properly human life which it involved. This emotional fracturing both within

69

himself and in his responses to the world beyond himself constitutes the thematic nucleus of *The Road to Wigan Pier*.

One of the several consequences of this division, and it seems to have been the most perturbing, is a peculiarly intense revulsion from the physicality of life and from the human body. Orwell himself insists on this as one of the effects of middle-class conditioning at that time. But his continual returning to this particular issue and the excess of examples provided suggest a compulsion that bears little relation to the requirements of a definition of exclusively class experience. At work here is surely something far deeper, a manner of perceiving that makes for a thorough-going disgust at life, a disgust that Orwell tells us affected him throughout his childhood and during his time in Burma as an Imperial policeman and that even now (if we can judge from some of the writing in this book) still retains a certain latent power. Here are a few instances of this characteristic insistence. First a well remembered experience from childhood days:

> You watched a great sweaty navvy walking down the road with his pick over his shoulder; you looked at his discoloured shirt and his corduroy trousers stiff with the dirt of a decade; you thought of those nests and layers of greasy rags below, and, under all, the unwashed body, brown all over (that was how I used to imagine it), with its strong, bacon-like reek. You watched a tramp taking off his boots in a ditch—ugh!

And here a sharply detailed memory from a later period:

> Once when I was thirteen, I was in a train coming from a market town, and the third class carriage was packed full of shepherds and pigmen who had been selling their beasts. Somebody produced a quart bottle of beer and passed it round; it travelled from mouth to mouth to mouth, everyone taking a swig. I cannot describe the horror I felt as that bottle worked its way towards me. If I drank from it after all those lower-class male mouths I felt certain I should vomit; on the other hand I dared not refuse for fear of offending them . . .

And here finally is a recollection of a time when Orwell as a young man was temporarily attached to a British regiment in Burma.

Of course I admired and liked the private soldiers as any youth of twenty would admire and like lofty, cheery youths five years older than himself and with the medals of the Great War on their chests. And yet, after all, they faintly repelled me; they were "common people" and I did not care to be too close to them. In the hot mornings when the company marched down the road, myself in the rear with one of the junior subalterns, the steam of those hundred sweating bodies in front made my stomach turn. And this, you observe, was pure prejudice. For a soldier is probably as inoffensive physically as it is possible for a male white person to be. He is generally young, he is nearly always healthy from fresh air and exercise, and a vigorous discipline compels him to be clean. But I could not see it like that.

A great deal of space in this book is devoted to Orwell's period in Burma. After all it marked the most important stage in his adult life. Here he became irrevocably convinced of the deadening effects of English middle-class style and of the imperial order which formed part of it. And here he rejected "that evil despotism" and became conscious of the "immense weight of guilt I had got to expiate". Orwell's many insights into the imperial mind in its final phase of enervation are all extremely fascinating, but they provide no convincing explanation of the primary fact of his own peculiarly complex guilt. Perhaps this major experience of his life will never be conclusively explained. Nevertheless we can extend our understanding of it if we return to the theme of life-nausea as it is continued in the Burmese section of the autobiography. This issue is not to the forefront of Orwell's declared intention; but it intrudes very strongly into the writing and implies a fundamental emotional change which may be anterior to and may even account for the changes in attitude and ideas which are the ostensible topic. "The essential point," Orwell observes when he suddenly and quite unexpectedly returns to this subject, "was that the 'natives', at any rate the Burmese, were not felt to be physically repulsive." He then proceeds in terms of very intimate memories to explain this awareness of a new possibility in perceiving and in responding to the human body.

One looked down on them as "natives", but one was quite ready to be physically intimate with them; and this I noticed was the case even with white men who had the most vicious colour-prejudice. When you have a lot of servants you soon get into lazy habits, and I habitually allowed myself, for instance, to be dressed and undressed by my Burmese boy. This was because he was a Burman and undisgusting; I could not have endured to let an English manservant handle me in that intimate manner. I felt towards a Burman almost as I felt towards a woman.

There then follows a long section in which Orwell makes detailed comparisons between the attractiveness of the Oriental body and that of the white man. "Admittedly," he concludes, "the white races throw up a few individuals who are supremely beautiful; but on the whole, say what you will, they are far less comely than Orientals." It seems very likely that this new ability to see sensuous beauty in man helps to explain Orwell's guilt at being a part of the imperial administration. Certainly it is the images of the specifically physical punishment meted out brutally and relentlessly to Burmese prisoners (punishment in which Orwell himself participated) which convey the most specific, the most vivid occasions of guilt which is elsewhere explained only in very general terms. "The wretched prisoners squatting in the reeking cages of the lock-ups, the grey cowed faces of the long-term convicts, the scarred buttocks of the men who had been flogged with bamboos, the women and children howling when their menfolk were led away under arrest—things like these are beyond bearing when you are in any way directly responsible for them." "Innumerable remembered faces—faces of prisoners in the dock, of men waiting in the condemned cells, of subordinates I had bullied and aged peasants I had snubbed, of servants and coolies I had hit with my fist in rage (nearly everyone does these things in the East, at any rate occasionally; Orientals can be very provoking)—haunted me intolerably."

Critics have commented upon the possible significance of the Orient upon Orwell's attitude to poverty and to the significance of a man's name. I think we may also say that Burma had a strong and curative effect on his long-standing disgust at man's physical nature. For there he learned both to admire the human body and to be horrified at the sight of its suffering under the unfeeling "mockery of so-called justice". Burma marks the stage at which Orwell began to be reconciled with that natural and physical world from which he believed himself to have been abruptly withdrawn in childhood and which for so long he had apprehended from a distorting perspective. Orwell is sometimes criticised for the insistence in his books upon the physically disgusting; but this is something which I think we must regard as a continuous nervous retesting of the power of old and consciously discarded ways of perceiving the world. The growing point of his life and work is his endeavour to validate that altogether different response which he first experienced in Burma. Moments of joyful physical contact are always carefully recorded throughout the autobiographies. In *Homage to Catalonia*, for instance, there are the profoundly significant handshakes with the Italian militia men at the beginning of the book and with the little colonel at the end. The moment of Orwell's ritualistic acceptance into the ranks of the down-and-out comes when the drunken stevedore in a lodging-house in Limehouse "collapsed on my chest and flung his arms round my neck. 'Ave a cup of tea, chum,' he cried tearfully, 'ave a cup of tea!'" And there are similar moments of pleasure in the physicality of life during Orwell's stay in Lancashire. There is, we note, no longer any disgust at the bodies of working men as Orwell watches the miners hard at work in the pit.

> It is only when you see miners down the pit and naked that you realise what splendid men they are. Most of them are small (big men are at a disadvantage in that job) but nearly all of them have the most noble bodies; wide shoulders tapering to slender supple waists and small pronounced buttocks and sinewy thighs, with not an ounce of waste flesh anywhere. . . . You can never forget that spectacle once you have seen it—the line of bowed kneeling figures, sooty black all over, driving their huge shovels under the coal with stupendous force and speed.

And this description of natural life, clearly seconded by the influence of D. H. Lawrence who serves as an important reference point in this book, reflects the same sort of acceptance and wonder:

> Although the snow was hardly broken the sun was shining brightly, and behind the shut windows of the carriage it seemed warm. According to the almanac this was spring, and a few of the

birds seemed to believe it. For the first time in my life, in a bare patch beside the line, I saw rooks treading. They did it on the ground and not, as I should have expected, in a tree. The manner of courtship was curious. The female stood with her beak open and the male walked round her and appeared to be feeding her. I had hardly been in the train half an hour, but it seemed a very long way from the Brookers' back kitchen to the empty slopes of snow, the bright sunshine and the big gleaming birds.

The main significance, in fact, of *The Road to Wigan Pier* is that it is a rewriting of personal history in such a way as to confirm both the release from existential nausea and the possibility of restoring emotional integrity. And this sense of reconciliation with the physical is the fundamental impulse behind all the other forms of reconciliation which the book proposes. Some of these are not easily realised. Though Orwell is able to overcome the problem of disunity within the self, there still remains, for instance, the complementary problem of achieving a more satisfactory reconciliation between the self and the outside world. If he is able to define a proper state of mind and feeling in terms of images and memories, there still remains the problem of the further regeneration of that mind through satisfying emotional relationships with others. And here his native class has absolutely nothing to offer; it is, he maintains, "a deadly net of frustration in which it is harder and harder to persuade yourself that you are happy, active or useful." For Orwell the only social embodiment of the natural unified life to which he can refer is the working class. Significantly, it is a sense of unity and completeness that informs Orwell's metaphors of that particular social ethos; we remember, for instance, his impression of the 'peculiar easy completeness, the perfect symmetry as it were of a working-class interior at its best". Nevertheless at the same time that he dwells on these images of the good life, Orwell is fully aware of his estrangement from it. As he remarks on one occasion, "the working-class home is a good place to be in provided that you can be not only in it but sufficiently of it to be taken for granted." This discrepancy between image and actuality is the main theme of all that follows in the book. Fully aware of the futility of personal gestures towards "class-breaking", Orwell turns in his later chapters to a set of proposals for a wider reconciliation between middle class and working class. It is to this that he refers when he speaks of "Socialism". Yet these chapters, coming after the long essay in autobiography, strike us as something more than political proposals. They are really proposals for a unity in social life that will be a counterpart to and an extension of the personal, psychological unity considered earlier. The same holds true for the account of contemporary literary culture which is another prominent feature of the later part of the book. For in his discussion of the lack of emotional range and depth in modern writing, Orwell is treating precisely the same problem that underlies his political proposals, namely his sense of the compartmentalisation and emotional restrictedness of English life as a whole.

Orwell's emphasis on the enervation of the English middle class during this particular phase of its three-century history and especially his hope for its regeneration through an accommodation with the working class have been found embarrassing by some of his more confidently middle-class contemporaries who have written about him. For us today, aware of a middle class with a new mood, new recruits and a new style, and seemingly closer to the working class by virtue of a "pop" culture that is in no way the popular culture that Orwell had in mind, his attitudes and experiences must seem those of a bygone age. They do not therefore today compel such defensive responses. Nonetheless we can see that at times Orwell's cult of the proletariat does come close to the sentimental. His recollection, say, of "winter evenings after tea, when the fire glows in the open range and dances mirrored in the steel fender, when Father, in shirt sleeves, sits in the rocking chair at one side of the fire reading the racing finals, and Mother sits on the other with her sewing, and the children are happy with a pennorth of mint humbugs, and the dog lolls roasting himself on the rag mat" cannot but strike us as an indulgence in a rather sugary stereotype. However, to remark upon the occasional unintelligence of the feelings expressed (and it is not only the working class which elicits such feeling) and to let this remark stand as an unqualified value statement is to do an injustice to the autobiographies. In the first place, we can see now that this lack of authenticity in his emotional life is something of which Orwell himself is very much aware. The story he has to tell is essentially that of a man seeking urgently to rid himself of the sham feeling that can express itself as sentimentality and to be enriched by genuine emotional experience. And secondly, we can also see from our present perspective in time that his concern with the problem of what constitutes true and proper feeling is the thing which most obviously relates Orwell's work to that of his contemporaries. For though his difficulties in this regard may be attributed in part to his own deficiences as a writer, they must also be seen to derive from the general emotional condition of the time. If for a moment we compare Orwell's writing with that of other thirties writers, we see that neither his difficulties nor his failures were peculiar to him. After all, this was the decade we associate with the often glibly ironic evasions of feeling in the poetry of W. H. Auden, with the often feigned and asserted emotional richness in the poetry of Dylan Thomas and with the comedy of well-mannered, poker-faced acceptance of gross emotional impropriety in the early novels of Anthony Powell. This decade also produced Elizabeth Bowen's *Death of the Heart*, a novel whose title and temper are perhaps the most symptomatic of all. The lack of dexterity with the life of feeling which we have observed in Orwell is as much of the generation as it is of the man.

It is also worth going on to suggest that if Orwell's particular type of emotional unsurety strikes us as being typical of the period, then his most natural form of expression, the autobiography, is similarly representative. Mainly as a result of the prominence of the Auden school of poetry, we have been accustomed to regard the main literary mode of the thirties as a poetry of social and political consciousness. However, as we look more closely at those years it becomes clear that prose autobiography is at least equally important as a characterising form of expression. Autobiography, we come to see, is the form which the second generation of modern English writers chose to employ to further their understanding of that nexus of problems involving the idea of the self, proper modes of selfhood and a new propriety of the emotions, as formulated and bequeathed by the first generation of moderns of the historic decade of the nineteen-tens. To these fundamental concerns of the century some of the most mature literary works of the thirties such as Edwin Muir's

The Story and the Fable (1940), R. G. Collingwood's *Autobiography* (1939) and Herbert Read's *Annals of Innocence* (1940) directly relate. This autobiographical impetus in the second phase of English *Modernismus* also seems to have affected writers of earlier generations. For during these years there also appeared H. G. Wells's *Experiment in Autobiography*, Wyndham Lewis's *Blasting and Bombardiering*, Ford Madox Ford's *It Was the Nightingale* and Norman Douglas's *Looking Back*, as well as Christopher Isherwood's *Lions and Shadows* and Arthur Koestler's *Scum of the Earth*. Nor was this sudden concern with the nature of the self confined exclusively to serious writers. Their work was but one expression of a concern that permeated English life generally. For a sudden spate of autobiographical writing is one of the most striking features of the literary culture as a whole during these years. In Malcolm Muggeridge's words, they produced autobiographies "by burglars, waiters, taxi-drivers, convicts, undergraduates, society ladies, diplomats, journalists, restaurateurs, politicians, down and outs, nomads, all conditions of men and women. . .". Muggeridge adds, "From the abundance of contemporary autobiography dealing with high and low but seldom middle-life a generation's aspirations may be deduced; all they would have wished to be and are not, all they might have experienced and have not."[46] To this general impulse of the time Orwell's autobiographies must be seen to relate. They treat of the same lack of self-confidence, the same vital exhaustion, the same sense of unformed emotion which is to be found in, and which indeed explains the very existence of, so many of these other essays in self-definition.

However, while Orwell's work bespeaks the general condition of the decade, it also reveals a moral urgency and a seriousness that is rare among his contemporaries. And if it is a statement of Orwell's many limitations to say that he was a man of his generation, then it is also a statement of his achievement to say that in terms of that generation his works stand out conspicuously as those of one who was genuinely and responsibly engaged in experience. If, for instance, we compare Orwell's three books with Christopher Isherwood's autobiography, *Lions and Shadows*, of 1938, we find the same basic emotional situation,

[46] Muggeridge, p. 38.

the same anxiety with regard to the self. (Incidently, Isherwood attributes this anxiety to the fact that his and Orwell's generation did not participate at all in the determining experience of the first World War.) But we also find, and this is the all important difference, that in Orwell's books there is a deeper and more sustained and more admirable effort to restore the self; there is none of Isherwood's tendency to retreat into anecdotal trivia and rueful self-depreciation. A different perspective upon the special quality of Orwell's work is provided when we compare it with J. B. Priestley's sequence of books, *English Journey* (1934), *Midnight on the Desert* (1937) and *Rain Upon Godshill* (1939), which like Orwell's three books form a serialised autobiography. *English Journey* in particular shows many points of resemblance with *The Road to Wigan Pier*. Its subtitle describes it as "Being a rambling but truthful account of what one man saw and felt and thought during a journey through England during the autumn of the year 1933". And besides the sounds and sights and thoughts and feelings, it also contains, like Orwell's book, the sort of documentary reporting and discussion of the condition of England question so characteristic of the time. But though they share the same subject and the same conventions, the effect of the two books is altogether different. In part this may be due to the different conditions of the two journeys. Priestley, unlike Orwell, was already a literary celebrity in the thirties. And he travels through England in a chauffeur-driven car, stays at large though (as he tells us) not always satisfactory hotels, spends money freely and has contacts with many influential citizens who provide him with hospitality and information. But the more crucial difference is in the responses of the two writers to what they see. For sheer comprehensiveness in the reporting Priestley's must be adjudged the superior book. He covers more of England and has access into many and various types of home and working life. He gives us long accounts of pottery manufacture and of car factories and chocolate factories and typewriter factories and of fairs and football matches and whist drives. But such descriptions are offered to us as being of interest merely in themselves. They are, we feel, of little but passing interest to Priestley. Certainly they are not informed or directed by any great personal concern on his part. And the result is that at times the prose becomes astoundingly slack and stale. Here, for example, are Priestley's feelings about Bristol:

It may be the fine weather or my own optimism, but my impression of the folk here—especially the working folk—is that the females are above the average in good looks and that the men are above the average in breadth of shoulder and stockiness. There is plenty of good old West Country blood about. You could pick a splendid revue chorus or a sound rugger side out of the nearest street. I feel that the working people here enjoy life. There is not that terrible dreariness which is probably the chief curse of our provincial towns. The people are hearty creatures who like to eat and drink well, and enjoy themselves.[47]

Like Orwell, Priestley is also concerned with the economic and social dislocation of English life at this time. But this too is something which he observes and comments upon from a distance. In his accounts of the stunted and stultified lives of those in the depressed areas, there is none of Orwell's profound involvement. Priestley's journey elicits from him nothing beyond mere opinion, opinion that is often rhetorically expressed:

Was Jarrow still in England or not? Had we exiled Lancashire and the North-east coast? Were we no longer on speaking terms with cotton weavers and miners and platers and riveters? Why had nothing been done about these decaying towns and their workless people? . . . Why has there been no plan for these areas, these people? The dole is part of no plan; it is a mere declaration of intellectual bankruptcy. You only have to spend a morning in the dole country to see that it is all wrong. Nobody is getting any substantial benefit, any reasonable satisfaction out of it. Nothing is encouraged by it except a shambling dull-eyed poor imitation of life. The labour exchanges stink of defeated humanity. The whole thing is unworthy of a great country that in its time has given the world some nobly creative ideas.[48]

[47] J. B. Priestley, *English Journey* (London, 1934), p. 28. The Georgian sentiment resorted to here is very reminiscent of that in Arthur Mee's multivolumed account of *The Kings England*, itself an interesting monument of one kind of thirties style and feeling in reportage.
[48] Priestley, p. 411.

79

These two passages from *English Journey* serve with perhaps an excess of clarity to illuminate what is living and distinguished in Orwell's book. For despite the gaucheries of feeling in *The Road to Wigan Pier*, there is feeling in it. It possesses a vitality and responsiveness such as are nowhere to be found in Priestley's account of his journey. By this I mean not so much that Orwell is politically or compassionately involved but rather that the paralysis of the North of England is seen by him as part of the same paralysis which he knows in his own life. His book treats of more than externals and opinions about externals. It also involves an essay into the self. And it is the presence of this self with all its doubts and uncertainties which explains why this book and his other autobiographies continue to interest us long after the stories of the lives and journeys of other thirties' writers have fallen into neglect.

I want now to go back to the last few chapters of *The Road to Wigan Pier* in which Orwell turns to consider the state of English society and of English letters. His analysis of the literary culture of the time is of particular importance since it marks his very first treatment of a subject that will become increasingly prominent in his autobiography, especially in that part made up by his essay sequence. The most striking feature of this portion of the book is the anger and contempt in the writing. The literary world of the day was, it would seem, a world made up of "the Nancy poets" and people like "Comrade X, author of *Marxism for Infants*", a world in which highbrow literary success "means delivering yourself over to horrible campaigns of wire pulling and back stairs crawling" and "kissing the bums of verminous little lions". This sort of violence obviously suggests some very painful personal experiences of literary life. But it also involves something of more enduring interest—Orwell's bitter frustration at the failure of modern writers to deal seriously either with the to him paramount issue of social and cultural reconciliation or with the possibilities of extending and reunifying the emotional life which above all else this issue entails. It is to such emotional reconciliation that Orwell refers when he speaks of "Socialism". And we notice that he is especially concerned to attack those who claim or are claimed to be socialist writers. This is because their attitudes, which purport to be attitudes of reconciliation, are, in Orwell's view, finally bogus. They lack the most crucial constituent, an awareness of new possibilities of feeling. What passes for socialist writing is often an expression of altogether distorted feeling. "The underlying motive of many Socialists", he complains in one place, "is simply a hypertrophied sense of order", a desire "to reduce the world to something resembling a chessboard." The plays of George Bernard Shaw are cited, as a fine example of this. Shaw, Orwell suggests, had no real feeling for the important qualities of working-class people: "At best his attitude . . . is the sniggering *Punch* attitude; in more serious moments . . . he finds them merely contemptible and disgusting." Unadmirable feeling is also to be found in the works of Galsworthy, "a very fine specimen of the thin-skinned, tear-in-they-eye, pre-war humanitarian". H. G. Wells and Orwell's fellow autobiographer, Beatrice Webb, also receive irritable dismissal. And left-wing writers of more recent generations rate even less consideration than those of the earlier period. The writers who have been most creative in terms of literary art and most influential in the conditioning of a modern feeling are, he recognises, writers who are altogether unsympathetic to his particular preoccupations; and the only representatives of specifically socialist literature in his own generation are "W. H. Auden, a sort of gutless Kipling, and the even feebler poets who are associated with him". The bad temper which informs these value judgements derives most significantly from Orwell's sense of the triviality of contemporary literary culture. At the same time that in *The Road to Wigan Pier* he first becomes able to formulate what are for him the crucial issues of experience, he also becomes aware of the extent to which he is alone in these preoccupations. For the literary culture, far from being able to offer anything to which he may relate or refer, is seen to be an embodiment of the very restrictedness and shallowness of emotion which he finds so damaging. At this moment, Orwell's autobiography becomes consciously the story of a writer as well as of a man. For now the reintegration of the self necessitates also new definitions of the proper function of the literary intellectual. From now on until the very last essays, Orwell's fundamental concern with a unity of feeling in the self and in society involves him also in a continuing self-definition in terms of literary and

81

cultural criticism. This new dimension of autobiography is one of the most important developments in *The Road to Wigan Pier*.

Orwell's sense of isolation in the book is not absolute however. There is one writer who commands serious attention and who involves him in some significant though complex responses, and that is D. H. Lawrence. Throughout the book, Orwell's attitude to Lawrence is one of unqualified respect. His work is seen above all as embodying the qualities of working-class life and particularly of that one section of working-class life, namely the mining communities of the North, which Orwell had set out specifically to investigate and to experience. And Lawrence is not only a subject of the book, he is also, as we have already remarked, an important influence in the very writing. Perhaps the jeering contempt of some of Orwell's literary value judgements owes something to Lawrence. At any rate, Orwell is very familiar with the mocking poetry of Lawrence's last years. The poem "Oh you've got to be like a monkey" he actually reproduces in his text and considers at some length. But the very power of this sort of attack on the middle class is precisely what complicates Orwell's feelings about Lawrence. For though he is ready to concede the justice of the attack, though he admits that someone like Lawrence, struggling out of his own class in order to find "a wider freedom and a greater intellectual refinement", will find in the middle class only "a sort of hollowness, a deadness, a lack of any warm human feeling—of any real life whatever", he is also, as one now conscious of his own undeniable middle-class affiliations, considerably antagonised by it. As he says, "If you want to make an enemy of a man, tell him his ills are incurable." There is, therefore, a tension in Orwell's mind between his acceptance of Lawrence's criticism and a sense of the radical threat which this criticism entails for his own essential selfhood and for the all important quality of self-respect. For Orwell, in his sounding of new possibilities of human relationship, D. H. Lawrence serves as both a landmark and a peril. He confirms the need for regeneration, but he also brings home the problem of maintaining the autonomy of the self while at the same time making the self susceptible to regenerative influences. At one point Orwell speaks of his early knowledge of the working class as being "at a distance and through the medium of books".

The same seems to have been true of his time in the North of England. Furthermore, in his attempt to establish a closer human proximity, there appears to have been something analogous to his ambivalent response to the greatest of working-class writers. If as a man and as a writer Orwell is able to identify what for him constitutes the valuable, there still remains the problem of the forms of approach and the proper personal posture which will allow for reconciliation with it.

The only proposal that Orwell is able to offer in this regard involves a call for a new unity in social life as a whole. And though this proposal, which is what Orwell means by socialism, serves to remove the whole issue from the difficult personal level, the throb of personal urgency is still very pronounced in the writing. The socialism which Orwell recommends in these final chapters is defined mainly in negative terms. First of all, he tries to dissociate the word from "a picture of vegetarians with wilting beards, of Bolshevik commissars (half gangster, half gramophone), of earnest ladies in sandals, shock-headed Marxists chewing polysyllables, escaped Quakers, birth-control fanatics and Labour Party back stairs crawlers". Also he wants to get rid of "the stupid cult of Russia" and, more importantly, the identification of socialism with a commitment to technological progress and "the inhuman cult of machine efficiency". But it is noticeable that there is no detailed programme enunciated in the book. Insofar as socialism is for Orwell a specifically political prescription, it signifies an alliance between the working class and those of good will in the middle class. However, the main purpose of this alliance is neither to fight Fascism nor unemployment, but rather to serve as a first feasible step in eliminating the divisions which make for the breakdown of human contact. The prospect of such a unity accounts for the strong pulse of feeling in the peroration with which the book ends:

> And when the widely separate classes who, necessarily, would form any real Socialist party have fought side by side, they may feel differently about one another. And then perhaps this misery of class prejudice will fade away, and we of the sinking middle class—the private schoolmaster, the half starved free-lance journalist, the colonel's spinster daughter with £75 a year, the

jobless Cambridge undergraduate, the ship's officer without a ship, the clerks, the civil servants, the commercial travellers and the thrice-bankrupt drapers in the country towns—may sink without further struggles into the working class where we belong, and probably when we get there it will not be so dreadful as we feared, for, after all, we have nothing to lose but our aitches.

The socialism preached in *The Road to Wigan Pier* is in essence a solution, couched in political terms, to the chief dilemma of Orwell's own life. It is not so much a political system as the prospect of a unity of being in society that will promote a similar unity within the self. It is a means to be rid of "the curse of class difference" which "confronts you like a wall of stone", "this perpetual uneasiness between man and man from which we suffer in modern England".

Orwell was to find what he was looking for not in modern England, but in Spain. The months that he spent there during the Civil War fighting with the anarchist militia were, despite great physical discomfort and the fact of being wounded, the high point of his recorded experience. And the sudden happiness which he knew there accounts for the memorable quality of his book about his time in Spain, *Homage to Catalonia*. Laurence Brander has called this work "the happiest and richest book he wrote, the longest and most satisfying of his autobiographies", and his comment suggests the admiration that informs most of of the published discussion of the book.[49] In this volume of autobiography one feels that Orwell has at last something to write about; that whereas the two preceding ones express the sense of being cut off from life and experience, the final one conveys a deep feeling of involvement with people and with a community. Because *Homage to Catalonia* is an attempt to define and to understand a distinct and unified experience, this book has a unity and an organising principle that is lacking in the other two. In them we are sometimes led to think that we are reading a series of essays loosely strung together, that Orwell has

[49] Brander, p. 21.

no sustained vision or argument to offer us, just a set of brief descriptions and comments. It is almost as though Orwell were writing for the sake of telling us that he has nothing vital to write about. Laurence Brander has seen *The Road to Wigan Pier* as but "a medley of documentaries and pamphlets", and the same could be said of *Down and Out in Paris and London*, containing as it does sketches of interesting "characters", anecdotes, the transcription of a folk song, an essay on oaths and slang, and a chapter of practical suggestions for the improvement of the casual wards of England.[50] But this is not the case with *Homage to Catalonia*. For here is a book which deals with and is inspired by an experience of such magnitude and importance for Orwell as to brook no sidetracking or padding.

In *Homage to Catalonia*, Orwell has three main purposes: to write a polemic, to report the Spanish Civil War as he saw it and to write, however hesitantly, the account of the succession of personal friendships and the state of emotional exhilaration which he enjoyed in Spain and which marked a turning point in his life. All three intentions dovetail into one another and the third subsumes and directs the others. The polemical writing is contained in the fifth and eleventh chapters of the book. In them Orwell seeks in considerable detail to refute the false or dishonest accounts of the Spanish Civil War that were published in the western press at the time. He sets out to demonstrate that the rising in Barcelona, in which he was both participant and witness, was not merely an act of resistance to Franco's revolution, but rather a left-wing revolution that aimed at setting up a socialist state under workers' control. At the same time, he attempts to expose the underhand methods by which the Communists, under instructions from Moscow, tried to discredit and to betray the rising in Barcelona. For the reader of today these polemical chapters are the least interesting. Orwell himself invites the reader to skip them, and at a rereading one is ready to accept the invitation; for the feuds, the coalitions and the interrelationships of the various political parties, all referred to confusingly by their initials, are immensely complex and of real interest only to the historian of the Spanish Civil War. And it must be noted that one recent historian has called in question

[50] Brander, p. 113.

85

the accuracy of what Orwell has to say in this regard.[51] This is not to accuse Orwell of dishonesty, for, as he himself remarked, "It is very difficult to write accurately about the Spanish Civil War, because of the lack of non-propagandist documents. I warn everyone against my bias and I warn everyone against my mistakes." However, the suspicion of inaccuracy and the occasional dullness in the chapters of polemic combine to make them the least living portions of the book. There are only two things in them that are worth talking about. In the first place, they show Orwell's first realisation of the difficulty of coming to a responsible opinion with regard to current events. The Spanish Civil War was a particularly glaring example of an episode the circumstances of which were so constantly and often wilfully misrepresented that responsible opinion in distant places could only be postponed or perhaps finally abdicated in favour of indifference. For the remainder of his life, after his return from Spain, Orwell was to continue to combat the growing tendency towards the perversion of information and the misuse of propaganda. In an essay such as "Politics and the English Language", and particularly in *Animal Farm* and *Nineteen Eighty-Four*, he again deals with nightmarish situations in which modern methods of communication and the perversion of the English language itself can prevent an apprehension of the factual, objective truth of a given event and thereby betray the human mind to the worst of Orwellian horrors, a web of unrealities.

The second interesting feature of the polemical chapters is related to the dominant autobiographical purpose of the book. For we can see that one motive for Orwell's desire to establish the truth about the war was his desire to vindicate the reputation of friends and acquaintances, the relationships with whom furnished the moment of rich experience that is his chief topic. He writes his polemic to defend people who represent courage, humaneness and decency against those who would slander and misrepresent them for political or personal advantage. With some emotion, Orwell refutes a certain journalist who "stated that the P.O.U.M. troops 'were playing football with the Fascists in no man's land' at a time when, as a matter of fact, the P.O.U.M. were suffering heavy casualties and *a number of my*

[51] see Hugh Thomas, *The Spanish Civil War* (London, 1961). p. 424.

personal friends were killed and wounded." (Italics mine.) And in another place he remarks that "It is not a nice thing to see a boy of fifteen carried down the line on a stretcher, with a dazed white face looking out from among the blankets, and to think of the sleek persons in London and Paris who are writing pamphlets to prove that this boy is a Fascist in disguise." The antithesis established in this sentence and set down with an anger which is scarcely controlled by the understatement of the first half dozen words is characteristic of the polemical sections of the book. The Spanish boy who was Orwell's comrade is there as a very vivid image. He is living, young, vulnerable and wounded. And the forces in modern life which threaten all that he is and represents are emblematised by "the sleek persons in London and Paris". Such people peddle abstraction, subserve inhuman ideology which denies the particularity of human life and feeling, and misrepresent the truth which is indispensable to proper communication and relationships.

Now if we see the underlying motive of Orwell's polemic to be the defence of certain friends and above all of his feeling for them, we must go on to say that in *Homage to Catalonia* the reportage, the second major element in the book, is often resorted to in order to escape from the need to express and to evaluate this feeling. Orwell is clearly at his most relaxed when giving meticulous descriptions of the day to day facts of his life at war. He takes an obvious pleasure in such things as a lengthy and detailed description of the badness of the militia's weapons or an account of the number of clothes that the body is able to wear under conditions of extreme cold. A preoccupation with the factual and impersonal characterises all the reporting in the book, whether it be a description of street fighting in Barcelona or an attack on a Fascist redoubt or even the very personal experience of being wounded. One reason for this determined objectivity is the desire to debunk all ideas of the glamour of warfare: "In war all soldiers are lousy, at least when it is warm enough." Throughout the book we are told of the physical discomfort of war, of its unheroism, its starkness, its horror and its indignities. This sort of emphasis is, of course, characteristic of much of the writing about war since warfare became mechanised; we are well acquainted with the same sort of thing in, for

87

example, Tolstoy's *Sebastapol Sketches,* in the poems of Wilfred Owen and in the novels of Erich Maria Remarque. Yet Orwell is unusually determined to dwell upon the sordid and the repulsive: "Into the cleft immediately behind the position all the refuse of months had been tipped—a deep festering bed of breadcrusts, excrement and rusty tins." I am sure there must be a dozen passages in the book which make the same sort of lingering allusion to the faecal and the squalid. Such insistence and overstatement testify to the same sort of nervousness on Orwell's part that we encountered before. Here perhaps they must also be seen as an attempt to present his credentials as someone who is "fully experienced", as one "who knows what he is talking about". Sometimes it seems as though Orwell were seeking to prove himself acquainted with the reality of harsh physical facts in order to lend authority to and to convince the reader of the validity of his account of more subtle and infinitely more valuable emotional experience, an account which he is shy about giving but which, at the same time, he is urgent to give. It may be that he is attempting to anchor himself in a detailed objectivity in order to prevent himself from drifting on what is for him an uncharted and imperfectly understood sea of complicated emotional experience. For his feelings, we notice, are in many respects contradictory. The Orwell who loftily pooh-poohs the idea of the glory of war must still confess that the sight of guns lashed to open railway trucks is a stirring one, "making one's heart leap as guns always do, and reviving that pernicious feeling, so hard to get rid of, that war *is* glorious after all". And when he first experiences trench warfare, encumbered as he is with rifle and sandbags, he cannot forbear to remark and to celebrate the thrill of real experience at last: "I even shouted to someone as we staggered along with a bag between us: 'This is war! Isn't it bloody?' "

There are, we come to feel, two levels of emotional response in the book, one belonging to the old and rejected world of Eric Blair and the other to the newly surmised world of George Orwell. And the reticence about the former carries over to all attempts to give expression to the latter. The result is that he is often ill at ease when trying to convey the all important intimations of new emotional possibilities. And hence the resorting to description of externals. Occasionally he is conscious of and articulate about this difficulty. In the last chapter of the book, for instance, he offers some comments which show his awareness of what was a major problem throughout his life. He writes: "I suppose I have failed to convey more than a little of what these months in Spain meant to me. I have recorded some of the outward events, but I cannot record the feeling they have left me with." However, although Orwell's insight into his difficulties in treating states of feeling is a sound one, his overall assessment of his achievement in this book is too pessimistic. Admittedly his success is partial and rather awkward, but it is nevertheless there, and this account of the education of the feelings, rather than the polemical chapters or the many passages of reporting, gives *Homage to Catalonia* its particular distinction.

The autobiographical intention of the book is established in the opening pages. Orwell begins by presenting a personal experience—his momentary meeting with an Italian militiaman at the barracks in Barcelona. The handshake and the brief conversation which the two shared were a memorable event. "It was," he writes, "as though his spirit and mine had momentarily succeeded in bridging the gulf of language and tradition and meeting in utter intimacy." He adds, "One was always making contacts of that kind in Spain." Indeed, descriptions of such encounters recur throughout the book. There are, for instance, the Spanish soldiers who give the wounded Orwell their whole ration of tobacco and the colonel who, in the last chapter, shakes hands with him in the most unpropitious circumstances. Of this latter incident Orwell writes, "I do not know if I can bring home to you how deeply that action touched me." But to the reader who has followed Orwell's career through the preceeding autobiographies, the importance of such moments is easily understood. These experiences in Spain are Orwell's eventual success in breaking out of isolation and in coming to the revitalising experience of human contact.

Such encounters not only have a powerful emotional impact and value in themselves; their effect is also enhanced by the fact that they were connected with and enacted within a whole way of life which was for Orwell an equally novel experience. When Orwell arrived in Barcelona in the late December of 1936, the town was under the control of the anarchists. All the shops and businesses had been collectivised. The streets were plastered with revolutionary posters. Waiters and shopworkers had discarded professional obsequiousness in favour of a more egalitarian attitude, and throughout the town there was a revolutionary excitement. "Above all," he writes, "there was a belief in the revolution and the future, a feeling of having emerged into an era of equality and freedom." "All this," he comments elsewhere, "was queer and moving." And we can readily appreciate that the first days in Barcelona provided Orwell with the things which he had sought after throughout his adult life—a sense of vitality, of fellowship and of community of purpose.

All this may seem uncomfortably close to the barricades romanticism to which left-wing intellectuals, and particularly those of the thirties, have been so prone. And Kingsley Amis in his *Socialism and the Intellectuals* has suggested that Orwell was as much a "romantic" as the other left-wing writers who were his contemporaries.[52] In respect to *Homage to Catalonia*, this is not true. For here we are not offered a dream world of proletarian solidarity either as a piece of self-indulgence or as a serious alternative to the status quo. In the first place, the Catalan revolution was no mere pipe dream; and in the second place, and more importantly, it is not presented as a political action which may and should be emulated, but rather as a moment of experience, as something fragile and ephemeral that eventually disappeared. In all his descriptions of the revolutionary society, Orwell insists upon what was for him its humane value, yet perceives and makes plain the extreme vulnerability of the impulse of human feeling upon which it is based. The shabby and illiterate militiaman is ultimately "pathetic" and so too are the Spaniards who laboriously spell out the words on the revolutionary ballad sheets in order to sing them. "There was," Orwell insists on reiterating, "something rather pathetic in the literalness with which these idealistic Spaniards took the hackneyed phrases of revolution."

The pathos devolves from the extreme fragility of the revolution. Not only was the surge of feeling which created the rising

[52] *The Beat Generation and the Angry Young Men,* ed. Feldman and Gartenberg (New York; Dell, 1958), p. 339.

unmaintainable over a long period of time, but also the forces of self-interest and political expediency were always ready to exploit, pervert, vilify or destroy it. And this, of course, is what finally happens. Here we must stress the design of Orwell's book, for *Homage to Catalonia* is so organised and structured as to emphasise this point with maximum force. The book divides readily into three sections. The first presents the revolution as Orwell observed it and was inspired by it in his first days in Barcelona; and the second describes his time at the front, where the same qualities of decency and humaneness continue to inform human relationships. This lasts until his return to Barcelona: "In the train all the way to Barcelona, the atmosphere of the front persisted; the dirt, the noise, the discomfort, the ragged clothes, the feeling of privation, comradeship and equality." Then in the third and final section, Barcelona is described as Orwell saw it on his return, four months later. Now the revolutionary atmosphere is dissipated, normal class divisions and class customs have reappeared, and the sort of life and relationships which Orwell had admired so much and from which he had derived so much have vanished. In their place is an atmosphere of political rivalry and hatred. Shortly after Orwell's return to the city, street fighting breaks out, and this confirms the end of what was for him the memorable moment. "I think few experiences could be more sickening, more disillusioning or finally more nerve-racking than those evil days of street warfare." The valuable experience was, as Orwell's design makes clear, a transitory experience. Indeed, the unsentimental insistence upon its transience is one of the ways in which its peculiar poignance is brought out.

The responsibility for the horrifying degeneration of the Catalan revolution is attributed by Orwell to the cynical policies of the Comintern. In the polemical chapters he devotes a great amount of space to exposing the dishonesty and the inhumanity of Communist policy. But these lengthy explanations are not responsible for the book's abiding literary interest. What is most valuable in this book about revolution has little to do with politics. What is most important is the account of the new and sudden insight into possibilities in human life that the experience of being in Spain offered. As Sir Richard Rees has said with reference to the description of Orwell's meeting with the Italian militiaman, "This is the first occasion in any of Orwell's books on which one feels that he really looked at and saw and paid attention to another human being. By paying attention I mean becoming aware of a man's *essence* instead of merely observing him from the outside as a bundle of characteristics and humours."[53] This new way of seeing and of relating to people became possible only in the atmosphere of comradeship which was a part of the same short lived outburst of human feeling that had its political manifestation in revolution. As a polemicist Orwell defends the human decency that was politically exterminated by the Communists. Much more importantly, as an autobiographer he tries to convey the feeling which created the revolution and also the value of the experience as he himself participated in it. Orwell celebrates a moment of vivid personal feeling, and this is the force of the word "Homage" in the title of the book. Furthermore, his assertion of emotional possibility involves an attack on those who would scorn it or conceptualise it out of existence, "the hard-boiled sneering civilisation of the English-speaking-races". Attempting to sum up the situation, Orwell writes, "One had been in a community where hope was more normal than apathy or cynicism, where the word 'comrade' stood for comradeship and not as in most countries for humbug."

The antithesis in this sentence in which hope, comradeship and community are opposed to cynicism, apathy and humbug is the major theme not only of *Homage to Catalonia* but also of the two preceding autobiographical volumes. But whereas in *Down and Out in Paris and London* and *The Road to Wigan Pier* Orwell's efforts to know the former and to rid himself of the latter had met with but partial success, here, in this third volume, a sense of possible richness and value in experience is at last fully achieved and triumphantly, if reticently, declared. This sense of abundant life is something which Orwell will not find easy to maintain throughout the remaining ten years of his life. This is clear from the subsequent autobiographical documents. Nevertheless, the moment in Spain will continue as an (indeed *the*) important reference point for Orwell in his future experiences.

[53] Rees, p. 65.

And for the reader too, it stands as the high point of Orwell's progress, being the occasion of the finest book that he wrote during the thirties. For both the writing and the quality of the experience described are manifestly of a higher order than anything in *Down and Out in Paris and London* or *The Road to Wigan Pier*. And we may surely add that of all the many works of literature in English inspired by the Spanish Civil War, there is none that is more moving or more memorable than Orwell's *Homage to Catalonia*.

4

The continuation of Orwell's autobiography is to be found in his essays. From around the time of the outbreak of the second World War until his death, that is to say throughout the second half of his writing life, the essay was the literary form which he most regularly employed. And of the thirty or so essays that make up the three collections, *Critical Essays* (1946), *Shooting an Elephant* (1950) and *England your England* (1953), all but two were written after 1939.[54] One reason that Orwell suddenly resorted to this form may have been the difficulties in book publication brought about by the war. However, if he did now become an essayist by necessity, he had always been one by nature. The autobiographies of the thirties are very much the work of a disguised essayist, each being made up of a sequence of distinct and only loosely related prose pieces. In them Orwell's characteristic method is to describe a particular experience and then to meditate, speculate or preach upon it. But he lacked the conviction and the energy to fuse these fragments into a whole. In *Homage to Catalonia* many of Orwell's uncertainties were swept away by a major emotional experience; and this book is the most unified of the autobiographies. But after his return to England Orwell was to undergo experiences that

[54] It is true that these volumes contain only a fraction of Orwell's prose pieces. He did, after all, live by his pen and served at times as a working journalist. But there is no doubt that these three collections, the first put together by Orwell himself and the latter two published posthumously, do contain the best of his short pieces. A more complete collection of Orwell's prose pieces is to be found in *George Orwell: The Collected Essays, Journalism and Letters*, edited by Sonia Orwell and Ian Angus (London, 1968).

undermined the confidence that he had gained in Spain. Throughout the forties new doubts, somewhat different from and much stronger than those of the thirties, beset him. And his autobiography again takes the form of a sequence of loosely related fragments. A sense of insoluble contradiction is the dominant feature of Orwell's life as it is recorded in the essay sequence. And this would seem to be the principal reason why he returned to this most provisional and tentative of literary forms.

Orwell's essays fall into three easily recognisable groups. The first comprises straightforward autobiographical essays such as "Shooting an Elephant", "How the Poor Die" and "Such, Such Were the Joys", in which Orwell describes important experiences in his early life. The second group contains essays in literary criticism. All criticism must to a greater or lesser extent tell us something of the critic; and in Orwell's case the literary criticism, or the cultural criticism as it might more appropriately be called, is often hard to distinguish from the autobiography. The authors he writes most successfully about are those such as Dickens and Wells whom he had admired since childhood. And what he says frequently tells us more about his own intellectual history than it does about the book in question. The third group of essays is more heterogeneous and less easy to define briefly. They are the essays which I shall call essays in current autobiography. They deal with the issues that concerned Orwell during the forties. They move from the reflections contained in "Looking Back on the Spanish War" to, among other things, considerations of the totalitarian impulse, the quality of modern intellectual life, the nature of modern art, nationalism, and the emergence of the new managerial society. They are all essays in thought. During the thirties Orwell had purposely sought the experience of action; but in the forties his life was, in comparison, sedentary and passive. These essays tell us very little of his everyday life. We do get a few brief glimpses; some essays refer to Orwell's wartime service in the Home Guard; others tell something of his work at the B.B.C. arranging broadcasts to India. But the important events in his life go unmentioned. The essays tell us nothing of the facts that we know about from other sources; for instance, the death of his first wife, his remarriage, his temporary emigration to the Hebrides. The autobiography contained in thesees says is intellectual autobiography. Read chronologically, as they are printed in the *Collected Essays*,[55] they form a continuous account of a man trying through thought, memories and books to resolve the ambivalences in his own mind and to come to terms with himself and his time.

I do not wish to insist too rigidly on this division of the essays into three groups. Very few of the essays fit perfectly into any single category; there is much overlapping. Many of the critical essays and reviews can easily be taken as essays in current autobiography, and there are those in this latter group which also tell much of Orwell's boyhood and early life. But if not altogether precise, these divisions are real, and they are useful in discussing Orwell's career as an essayist. Before looking at the essays in current autobiography, those that continue the story from where it left off in *Homage to Catalonia*, I want first to consider the more orthodox autobiographical essays. For these not only restate and broaden the account of himself given by Orwell in the books of autobiography, they also reveal very clearly the development of the characteristically Orwellian manner with the essay as a literary form.

The most striking feature of these essays on his past life is that when taken in proper sequence they show the same early infatuation with symbolist techniques and the same growing away from them that we have already observed in the novels and the autobiographies. The essay entitled "A Hanging", which was first published in *The Adelphi* as early as 1931, is a clear-cut example of the symbolist manner adopted by Orwell in his early writing. The essay is an account of the hanging of a Hindu prisoner in Burma at which Orwell assisted. The whole experience is vividly evoked, mainly through the effective use of adjective and metaphor. First he conveys the bizarre atmosphere

[55] This edition, though it claims to contain all the essays contained in the three volumes, *Critical Essays, Shooting An Elephant* and *England Your England*, does not in fact contain the three essays, "England Your England" (1941), "Rudyard Kipling" (1942) and "Reflections on Ghandi" (1949). Nor does it contain the important autobiographical essay "Such, Such Were the Joys".

of the early morning with a "sickly light, like yellow tinfoil", an atmosphere which is in keeping with the barely suppressed nervousness of the British officers and Indian jailers, who are all quickly established for us by the economical but effective use of dialogue. The warders handle the prisoner "like men handling a fish which is still alive and may jump back into the water". The nervous sense of terrible comedy that is registered in this simile pervades the whole essay. The prisoner has a large moustache "like the moustache of a comic man in the films". Orwell cannot forbear to think of the life processes going on within the man's body "in solemn foolery". The whole party waits edgily for the eight o'clock bugle to set in motion the formal procedure of the execution. The tense situation is suddenly exacerbated when a stray dog appears and threatens to disrupt the formalised march to the scaffold. This little incident is an intolerable harrassment for already ragged nerves; it was "a dreadful thing". The tension is brought virtually to breaking point when the prisoner begins "crying out to his god". "It was a high, reiterated cry of 'Ram! Ram! Ram! Ram!' not urgent and fearful like a prayer or a cry for help, but steady, rhythmical, almost like the tolling of a bell." The almost unbearable tension of the officials is released when, after the execution has at long last been performed, they are all seized by an uncontrolled levity. The relief is so great that strict taboos are momentarily forgotten and British officers and Indian N.C.O's converse, joke and even at the last have a drink together.

As the rendering of an experience the essay is impressive; and the critical acclaim that it has received is merited. For Tom Hopkinson, "the result — in spite of its tiny scale — is a complete work of art."[56] And for Laurence Brander, "It recalls in its deft lightness the best of D. H. Lawrence's descriptions of the human mystery."[57] This comparison with Lawrence is appropriate; indeed the essay invites it. For the main point is not so much the experience itself, but the experience as a state of mind, a state of mind in which Orwell comes to a new awareness. His chief purpose, and it is a symbolist purpose, is to convey a moment of realisation, an illumination, an epiphany. Nevertheless it seems to me that the obvious Laurentian element in the

[56] Hopkinson, p. 15.   [57] Brander, p. 91.

essay is a weakness and not a strength. The experience is finely conveyed, but the moment of illumination is less convincing. Here is how Orwell expresses it: "It is curious but till that moment I had never realised what it means to destroy a healthy, conscious man. When I saw the prisoner step aside to avoid the puddle I saw the mystery, the unspeakable wrongness, of cutting a life short when it is in full tide." The idiom here is familiar; "the mystery," "the unspeakable wrongness," "a life . . . in full tide" are all unmistakably Laurentian. But in terms of the language of the rest of the essay they are a supervention and do not enhance its effect. The atmosphere of tension and jangled nerves and the horror of waiting for the execution to take place all come across as things genuinely felt. By comparison, the moment of illumination seems asserted, out of place, just a matter of words, something which Orwell felt obliged to insert. We do not doubt Orwell's opposition to hanging, but we do doubt the actuality of the sudden overwhelming insight which he tries to describe. Here, as elsewhere in Orwell's writing, we can see the detrimental effect of the symbolist influence. It leads him to claim a type of feeling which he has not experienced, but which, in order to be a writer, he feels he ought to experience.

"Shooting an Elephant", one of Orwell's most famous essays, was first published in 1936, five years after "A Hanging". And it reveals some considerable development in Orwell's understanding of the essay form. The subject matter is still of the same sort. Orwell's main purpose is still to record a moment of sudden insight which he claims as an important stage in his education. The incident is well known; it begins when Burmese villagers call upon Orwell, the Imperial policeman, to deal with an elephant that has gone on the rampage. Tracking the animal down to a paddy field, Orwell finds that it is now much calmer and that its original attack of "must" is already passing off. His inclination is not to kill the elephant, but glancing around at the large crowd of Burmese that has followed him to see the killing, he realises that he has no choice. This is the moment of understanding:

> And it was at this moment, as I stood there with the rifle in my hands, that I first grasped the hollowness, the futility of the white man's dominion in the East. Here was I, the white man with his

gun, standing in front of the unarmed crowd—seemingly the leading actor of the piece; but in reality I was only an absurd puppet pushed to and fro by the will of those yellow faces behind. I perceived in this moment that when the white man turns tyrant it is his own freedom that he destroys. He becomes a sort of hollow, posing dummy, the conventionalised figure of a sahib. . . . He wears a mask, and his face grows to fit it.

As with the experience treated in "A Hanging", Orwell seeks to make this moment of insight, this painful realisation of the tension between the mask and the true self, something that the reader shall feel vividly. There are, for instance, the paragraphs which describe in harrowing detail the slow and tortured death of the elephant after the shots are fired. Nevertheless, if there are similarities between the two essays, the differences, particularly the differences in Orwell's literary approach to what is essentially the same sort of subject, are the more striking.

The five years that intervene between them signify a distinct moving away from a symbolist idea of the essay. Most obviously "Shooting an Elephant" is not intended as a work of art in the way "A Hanging" is. The earlier essay could very easily be taken by someone ignorant of its authorship as a short story or as a chapter from a novel. It is a rendering of an experience and it is to this and this alone that we are asked to respond. There is no mediation by commentary, discussion or editorial. The essay adheres to the famous injunctions of the dominant literary aesthetic: "Direct treatment of the 'thing' whether subjective or objective"; "To use absolutely no word that does not contribute to the presentation."[58] In "Shooting an Elephant" on the other hand, we are dealing unquestionably with an essay, with an example of that form which we can see evolving in English over three centuries. In "Shooting an Elephant" the incident related is not sufficient unto itself nor does it make its effect in the manner, say, of one of James Joyce's stories in *Dubliners*. The experience related is subsidiary and is merely used as an illustration by the essayist, whose voice and personality are the main matter of the piece. The experience is no

[58] Ezra Pound, "A Retrospect", *Literary Essays of Ezra Pound* (London, 1963), p. 3.

longer an image, but merely an anecdote that forms but part of a discourse on the contradictions in the author's thoughts and situation. It is just an illustration, something "which in a round-about way was enlightening". "Shooting an Elephant" is an essay in the very basic sense of being an attempt. It is a venture in explicating what is uncertain and doubtful.

At the outset the author's reflections upon his experiences are established as the subject of the essay. Here are two successive sentences each expressing one of the many ambiguities which the essay tries to resolve. "I did not even know that the British Empire is dying, still less did I know that it is a great deal better than the young empires that are going to supplant it. All I knew was that I was stuck between my hatred of the empire I served and my rage against the evil-spirited little beasts [the Burmese] who tried to make my job impossible." The nexus of ambiguities which forms the subject of the discussion extends also to the style of the essay. It begins with a sentence that suggests an ex-Colonial Office raconteur on the B.B.C. Home Service. "In Moulmein, in Lower Burma, I was hated by large numbers of people—the only time in my life that I have been important enough for this to happen to me." The tone, the appropriate modesty and the contrived opening all establish immediately the Old Etonian who will resort to some obvious Latin tags (*saecula saeculorum, in terrorem*) and who will be unable to resist indulging in a little parody of the way the Burmese describe the rampage of the elephant: "also it had met the municipal rubbish van, and, when the driver jumped out and took to his heels, had turned the van over and inflicted violences upon it." But inter-mingled with the language of the imperial official, there are phrases, sentences and a tone of voice that do not fit in with the other forms. There is the chatty, more immediate relationship with the reader ("Feelings like these are the normal by-products of imperialism; ask any Anglo-Indian official, if you catch him off duty"), there are the colloquial expressions ("chucked up my job", "got badly on my nerves") and there are passages in which violent feeling escapes from formal restraint (". . . I thought that the greatest joy in the world would be to drive a bayonet into a Buddhist priest's guts"). This sort of writing has a more modern, colloquial, plebeian quality to it. And the lack of stylistic unity in the essay is one expression of Orwell's complex attitude to his subject. Orwell wrote the piece some ten years after his service in Burma and though the resolution at which his essay arrives is a firm but delicate condemnation of imperialism, we can see both in what he says and in the way he says it the difficulties involved in taking such a position. For it entails a denunciation of part of himself, of his experience and background. The particular value of the essay as a literary form is that it allows the expression of all the contradictions in thought and feeling that may attend the crystallisation of moral attitudes. It makes room for all the hesitations that may precede and accompany conviction. "Shooting an Elephant" marks an important stage in Orwell's career because it shows his first discovery of a form appropriate to his needs. The earlier piece, "A Hanging", is unsatisfactory because the moment of illumination that it tries to assert implies a confidence about the nature of reality such as Orwell never possessed. In "Shooting an Elephant", where we see him anatomising his uncertainties, the effect is more convincing.

"Shooting an Elephant" is a transitional essay. It contains vestiges of the early symbolist manner, and it also points forward to the mature essays of the forties. In order to suggest something of Orwell's later development of this form, I want to consider one of his last essays in autobiography, "Such, Such Were the Joys", which in its form and organisation is an excellent example of the mature Orwellian essay. Its manner is typical of the forties essays whether in criticism or current autobiography.

The most immediately remarkable feature of "Such, Such Were the Joys" (and it is a very characteristic one) is the fact that it is divided into sections. There are six of them. At first sight such a division might seem to be a matter of punctuation, but on closer inspection we see that it is a consequence of the divisions in Orwell's own mind, a consequence of the old inability to synthesize experience. As in the earlier autobiographical volumes, there is in this essay that Orwell wrote at the end of his life[59] a conspicuous lack of unifying conviction and of

[59] Internal evidence suggest that the essay was written sometime in the late forties. Commenting on events that took place in 1916,

essential continuity. The essay strikes us not so much as an entity as six essays within an essay. It is true that in terms of what we may call content each section proposes a discussion of the same thing: the guilt and misery which Orwell underwent as a boy during his years at the preparatory school he calls Crossgates. But the approach to this experience in each of the six sections is different, and the effect of the essay as a whole—and this is the case with many of Orwell's essays—is to provide interpretations of the experience which not only differ but are to some extent contradictory.

The first section of the essay is an extremely personal document. It is one of the least reticent passages in all of Orwell's autobiographical writings. It describes his memories of his first days at Crossgates. A straightforward catalogue of the incidents recorded, the bed-wetting, the threats from the headmaster's wife, the beatings, the lunatic mishearings and misunderstandings, might suggest a tedious indulgence in self-pity. But this is far from the case. For though he succeeds in conveying very vividly the peculiar agony of those days of his childhood, Orwell is quite detached from the experience. The fact that he suddenly remembers these events intrigues him as much as the actual experiences themselves. He writes in the manner of someone ever so slightly bemused by an access of memory. He is obviously surprised by his clear and sudden recollection of "things which did not strike me as strange or interesting until quite recently", things which "lay unnoticed in my memory for twenty or thirty years". In the first section of "Such, Such Were the Joys" we see a particularly powerful manifestation of a tendency that is present throughout Orwell's forties essays whatever their immediate purpose—a tendency to recall and to dwell on his early life. Autobiography describes and interprets the past, but the very interpretation reveals something of the writer at the time of writing. And Orwell's sudden memories of Crossgates that are set forth in this section are not offered sentimentally, for their own sake. They are there as part of a very personal apologia, as documentation of "the great abiding lesson of my

Orwell remarks that "All this was thirty years ago and more." *Collected Essays*, p. 50.

childhood: that I was in a world where it was not possible for me to be good". This, at least, is the purpose and the direction which the first part suggests.

The opening pages conduct the reader *in medias res* by describing the childhood suffering. The second section of the essay turns away from this and provides both a general account of Crossgates, from an adult perspective, and an explanation of the reasons why Orwell found himself there. Some light relief is afforded by the amusing description of the education meted out at the school. For Sim, the headmaster, teaching was solely a matter of cramming boys so that they might win scholarships at famous public schools and thus add useful ornament to his school prospectus. Sim was particularly relentless in cramming boys like Orwell who had been admitted at reduced prices as good scholarship prospects. But the comic strain does not last long. Gradually the writing edges back to Orwell's personal difficulties: his deep anxiety about winning a scholarship, his occasional nervous inability to work, his failure to feel the gratitude which he was told and which indeed he believed he owed to Sim, his wild belief that all adults, even those in the outside world, were Sim's informers. But if the second section of the essay eventually resumes the subject proposed in the first, this subject no longer receives the prime emphasis. Orwell's account of the surreal and painful world of his school-days is now a secondary theme. The chief concern is no longer with Orwell personally but with the nature of childhood generally. The following sentences are typical of many that show the shift of interest in this section. "A child may be a mass of egoism and rebelliousness, but it has not accumulated experience to give it confidence in its own judgments. On the whole it will accept what it is told, and it will believe in the most fantastic way in the knowledge and power of the adults surrounding it." The two quite different intentions established in the first two sections of the essay continue to the end of it. The reader is never sure whether Orwell's purpose is to describe his childhood as a means of explaining himself or whether it is to consider childhood generally, using his own experiences much more modestly, for the sake of illustration only. We may express this bifurcation of purpose another way, by saying that Orwell seems uncertain whether the sufferings of his boyhood were the consequences of his own particular nature or whether such pain is the inevitable lot of any child.

Orwell's intention becomes even more uncertain when in the fifth section of "Such, Such Were the Joys" he places the experience of his school-days in a completely new perspective. He now suggests that his difficulties derived from the historical context, from the particular contradictions inherent in the Edwardian age, an age of which Crossgates was a microcosm. "The essential conflict was between the tradition of nineteenth-century asceticism and the actually existing luxury and snobbery of the pre-1914 age." In Orwell's view this conflict was resolved through the assimilation of the former by the latter. "The goodness of money was as unmistakable as the goodness of health or beauty, and a glittering car, a title or a horde of servants was mixed up in people's minds with the idea of actual moral virtue." In such a situation, the suggestion runs, it was inevitable that Orwell who "was weak," "was ugly," "was unpopular," who "had a chronic cough," who "was cowardly" and who, above all, "smelt" should be seen by himself and by others as doomed to failure. (It is interesting to note that even thirty years later it was something of a cathartic release for Orwell to rehearse these deficiencies; he is anxious to rebut any charge of exaggeration: "This picture, I should add, was not altogether fanciful. I was an unattractive boy.") Looking back on the Edwardian years of his boyhood, the adult Orwell evokes them in a language which evinces a strong puritanical and Jacobin scorn:

There never was, I suppose, in the history of the world a time when the sheer vulgar fatness of wealth, without any kind of aristocratic elegance to redeem it, was so obtrusive, as in those years before 1914. It was the age when crazy millionaires in curly top hats and lavender waistcoats gave champagne parties in rococo houseboats on the Thames, the age of diabolo and hobble skirts, the age of the 'knut' in his grey bowler and cut-away coat, the age of *The Merry Widow*, Saki's novels, *Peter Pan* and *Where the Rainbow Ends*, the age when people talked about chocs and cigs and ripping and topping and heavenly, when they went for divvy weekends at Brighton and had scrumptious teas at the Troc. From the whole decade before 1914, there seems to breathe forth a smell of the more vulgar, un-grown-up kinds of luxury, a smell of brilliantine and creme de menthe and soft centered chocolates— an atmosphere, as it were, of eating everlasting strawberry ices on green lawns to the tune of the Eton Boating Song.

The element of retaliation in this passage makes clear how very selective and particular was that view of the Edwardian era which served Orwell as a myth of the good life. "The England of my boyhood", which is so frequently a reference point in Orwell's thinking, was no immaculate golden age. For though there is, I think, even amidst all the contempt, some slight note of affection in this passage, there is no doubt that he now lays the blame for his childhood miseries upon certain aspects of that historical period which in other respects signified for him so much that was fine. He sees himself as a victim of the vulgar and supremely intolerant snobbishness of the Edwardian age, as a casualty of history.

In the last section of "Such, Such Were the Joys" Orwell reinforces this historical interpretation of his experiences when he suggests that a child's lot has probably improved now after thirty years or so, chiefly because of "a vast change of outlook, a general growth of 'enlightenment' even among ordinary, unthinking middle-class people". And yet this interpretation is no more conclusive than any of the others. At the very end of the essay the question still remains: does Orwell regard these particular experiences as the consequences of his own individual make-up or as the consequences of the historical situation or just as the suffering to which any child is prey? The easy and obvious answer is to say that all three make their contribution. But this is to ignore the precise effect which the essay as a whole has upon us. For the sectioning of the essay gives the impression of Orwell attempting each of these explanations without reaching any real conclusion and then abandoning it in order to try another. This failure to determine the meaning of experience is not a deficiency in the essay. I mention it for purposes of description rather than of criticism. It is in fact the sort of difficulty with which the essay as a form is especially suited to deal. And as an essay in autobiography "Such, Such Were the Joys" is especially interesting because it shows how even at the end of his life Orwell remained just as uncertain about the significance of experience and of the self as he had been in the earlier autobiographies. Are the self and its experience to be expressed because of their intrinsic value and importance or merely in order to document some larger matter such as "the general state of childhood" or "social change"? Is the self important because of its uniqueness or because of its representativeness? There are of course writers whose work subsumes and reconciles all these alternatives. But Orwell was not such a one. For him these questions remained unanswered.

Orwell's uncertainty derives in great part from his cultivation of democratic feeling. In the essays we can observe how this impulse, whose early history is related in the autobiographies, leads eventually to a rigid convention in the relations between Orwell and his readers. Orwell comes to be recognised, and also to feel his responsibilities, as the socialist writer. And this necessitates the curbing of any tendency such as we find in "Such, Such Were the Joys" to investigate the self for its own sake.[60] Indeed, in this essay as in others, reminiscences and speculations of a personal nature are made to serve a progressive, reformist purpose. And this we can see as a further (the fourth) intention of the essay. Here I am not talking so much about the bias against private education that runs through the essay, though the criticism of Crossgates is devastating in its fine satiric control. (One remembers, to take just one example, the quiet irony with which Orwell, almost parenthetically, tells us of Sim's diagnosis of Orwell's defective bronchial tubes as "wheeziness", "essentially a moral disorder caused by over-eating".) Much more insisted upon and perhaps less convincing is his account of the one lesson he claims he learned from his persecution at Crossgates and in particular from his dealings with the school bully. It is the lesson of how to solve "the moral dilemma that is presented to the weak in a world governed by the strong: Break the rules or perish." To the youthful in-experience that prevented him from understanding this essenti-ally socialist tenet, the adult Orwell now ascribes the misery of

[60] There are quite a few essays, especially among those written for *Tribune*, in which Orwell finds it necessary to defend himself against charges of reactionary subjectivism.

his schooldays. "I did not see that in that case the weak have the right to make a different set of rules for themselves; because, even if such an idea had occurred to me there was no one in my environment who could have confirmed me in it." At this point the essay begins to read very much like an argument for socialism. The personal experiences, it now seems, are offered only as a contribution towards substantiating the case. The essay is no longer primarily autobiography; it has become propaganda.

But this last of Orwell's several shifts of attitude and purpose is no more his final position than any of the others. For when we come to the sixth and final section of the essay, we find that Orwell has abandoned it. Indeed this last section offers no real conclusion at all. There are no clinching statements, no resolution of all the uncertainties that have gone before. The essay ends with what I shall call the device of the parenthetical or suspended conclusion. It is a device that needs to be named because it is typical of Orwell's manner with the essay form. At the end of "Such, Such Were the Joys" we encounter the same sort of evasiveness, the same abdication in the face of his contradictory views of experience that we shall find in all the major essays. Our first impression of the final section is that it is very much "tacked on". This impression is heightened as he moves unsequentially to some generalisations about the liberal tendencies in education over the last thirty years and thence to some comments upon the remoteness from adult experience of the world of childhood. At one point the ending degenerates into mere chat when Orwell gives an example of a particularly gratuitous act of cruelty to a child. It is "a case not known to me personally, but known to someone I can vouch for. . . ." Thereafter the essay briefly rehearses some of the interpretations of his schooldays made earlier and then concludes abruptly with a personal and somewhat elegiac paragraph.

In a way it is only within the last decade that I have really thought over my schooldays, vividly though their memory has haunted me. Nowadays, I believe, it would make very little impression on me to see the place again, if it still exists. And if I went inside and smelt again the inky, dusty smell of the big schoolroom, the rosiny smell of the chapel, the stagnant smell of the swimming bath and the cold reek of the lavatories, I think I should only feel what one invariably feels in revisiting any scene of childhood: How small everything has grown and how terrible is the deterioration in myself!

The essay begins and ends as an essay in personal feeling. But it is the intervening and always unsuccessful attempts to discover the proper perspective on such feelings that makes this a characteristic essay. "Such, Such Were the Joys" is one of the most revealing chapters in Orwell's autobiography, not only for what it tells us of his life but also for what it reveals of his difficulties in understanding his life. There is no other piece, I think, which demonstrates more clearly or more succinctly the fundamental uncertainties in his mind, nor is there any other piece which better shows how his fragmented view of experience conditioned his manner with the essay. The craft of the essay, misunderstood in "A Hanging" but in "Shooting an Elephant" already maturing, is in "Such, Such Were the Joys" at the highest point to which Orwell was able to develop it. The Orwellian form is here fully achieved.

Of the remaining essays in what I have called straightforward autobiography there is only one, "How the Poor Die", that I want to say anything about. It is not an especially distinguished essay, and I mention it only because it makes for an easy transition to the essays in literary criticism and because it is an excellent example of the way Orwell's history was a continual interaction of reading and of direct experience. It is the best single piece of evidence of the inseparability of Orwell the autobiographer and Orwell the student of literature. The essay is something of a supplement to *Down and Out in Paris and London*. It begins as the story of Orwell's horrible experiences in a Paris hospital in 1929. There is a succession of comic grotesque descriptions of the poor and underprivileged who were Orwell's fellow patients, and he compares the inhuman indifference towards the chronically ill in that hospital with the more humane treatment afforded by English hospitals. But his sardonic telling of particularly gruesome hospital stories is not the main part of the essay. What most fascinates Orwell is the way that hospital brought back and confirmed all the horrors of Victorian infirmaries that he had read about as a child, especially in Tennyson's "The Children's Hospital":

> It happened that as a child I had had it read aloud to me by a sick-nurse whose own working life might have stretched back to the time when Tennyson wrote the poem. The horrors and sufferings of the old-style hospitals were a vivid memory to her. We had shuddered over the poem together, and then seemingly I had forgotten it. Even its name would probably have recalled nothing to me. But the first glimpse of the ill-lit murmurous room, with the beds so close together, suddenly roused the train of thought to which it belonged, and in the night that followed I found myself remembering the whole story and atmosphere of the poem, with many of its lines complete.

What is intriguing here to Orwell the autobiographer is the working of the memory. The reader may find it less interesting and conclude that this is a very slight essay. Nevertheless, it provides some useful information about the childhood reading that significantly affected the development of Orwell's mind. Above all this essay shows how very widely read he was in the fiction of the nineteenth century and how deeply affected he was by the grotesque and the horrific in those novels:

> From the nineteenth century you could collect a large horror literature connected with doctors and hospitals. Think of poor old George III, in his dotage, shrieking for mercy as he sees his surgeons approaching to 'bleed him till he faints'! Think of the conversations of Bob Sawyer and Benjamin Allen, which no doubt are hardly parodies, or the field hospitals in *La Debacle* and *War and Peace*, or that shocking description of an amputation in Melville's *Whitejacket*! Even the names given to doctors in nineteenth-century English fiction, Slasher, Carver, Sawyer, Fillgrave and so on, and the generic nickname "sawbones", are about as grim as they are comic.

"About as grim as they are comic." These words are just as applicable to the outlines of the world that Orwell, reared on Victorian fiction, was to see throughout his life. The books that he read as a child became a part of himself and of his outlook. And this is why, when he writes about them, his subject is as much himself as the given work or author. And of course it is a fact that Orwell's best critical essays are on those very books that he had cherished since childhood. In them the autobiographical concern is always explicit. In the well-known essay on Charles Dickens he notes that "Before I was ten years old I was having Dickens ladled down my throat . . .", and that "I must have been about nine years old when I first read *David Copperfield*. The mental atmosphere of the opening chapters was so immediately intelligible to me that I vaguely imagined they had been written by a child." In "Politics vs. Literature" there is a good example of how the peculiarly personal significance of a book (in this case *Gulliver's Travels*) is established in terms of even more detailed memories: "I read it first when I was eight—one day short of eight, to be exact, for I stole and furtively read the copy which was to be given to me next day on my eighth birthday—and I have certainly not read it less than half a dozen times since." And here is one further instance of the way in which certain books and writers stand as major items in Orwell's autobiography. It is taken from the essay "Wells, Hitler and the World State".

> Back in the nineteen-hundreds it was a wonderful experience for a boy to discover H. G. Wells. There you were, in a world of pedants, clergymen and golfers, with your future employers exhorting you to 'get on or get out', your parents systematically warping your sexual life, and your dull-witted schoolmasters sniggering over their Latin tags; and here was this wonderful man who could tell you about the inhabitants of the planets and the bottom of the sea, and who *knew* that the future was not going to be what respectable people imagined.

This strong and ever present autobiographical concern conditions Orwell's criticism in both its range and method. If we discount the slighter, less thought-out essays Orwell wrote in his capacity as a reviewer, we see that his critical interests were extremely limited. Except for those on Swift and Shakespeare none of the major literary essays deals with anything outside the Victorian and Edwardian periods. And even within this span of time Orwell's interests are highly selective. He is deeply read in Dickens and Thackeray, in Chesterton and Wells; he is able to make easy and knowledgeable reference to very minor Victorian works such as *Mr. Verdant, Frank Fairleigh, Mrs. Caudle's Curtain*

Lectures and *The People of Clopton*, and he is familiar with the work of a host of minor Edwardians—Gunby Hadath, Surtees, Desmond Coke, Sax Rohmer; and yet, rather surprisingly, of two major writers of this time, George Eliot and Henry James, he has nothing to say. In terms of the standard contemporary view of the literature of the last hundred and fifty years or so these predelictions seem eccentric. Nevertheless they amount to a form of literacy which we can recognise. We are still close enough to the Edwardian period to know that the range, if not the depth, of Orwell's reading corresponds to what may be called Edwardian middle-class taste. Such taste extends to the more intellectually accessible Victorian classics but also takes great pleasure in "a type of book . . . which flowered with great richness in the late nineteenth and early twentieth centuries, . . . what Chesterton called 'the good bad book': that is, the kind of book that has no literary pretensions but which remains readable when more serious productions have perished." The "good bad book" and the "good bad poem" are prominent concepts in Orwell's thinking about literature. They are important to him as means of justifying literary admirations which the critical intelligence cannot support. It was not Orwell's purpose to try to define the best that is known and thought. Nor was he a disciplined or in any way a systematic critic. To recall Ezra Pound's endeavour to make value judgements in terms of world literature or F. R. Leavis's interpretation of the whole corpus of English literature is to realise how very slight, how very parochial Orwell's criticism is. His critical essays at their best are but discussions of books that happen to have been important in his personal development particularly, those books that were to hand in his boyhood.

Orwell's manner of critical proceeding reveals the same peculiarly and unashamedly personal preoccupations. The most immediately striking feature of his criticism is that he rarely writes about a given literary work. His preference is to write about the author as an embodiment of certain attitudes and values. Orwell is usually concerned with a writer's "position" and with the extent to which that position is coincident with his own. And this position is seldom defined in terms of the language that is used or in terms of the aesthetic experience which any given work may afford. Rather it is expressed as generalisations extrapolated from a whole *oeuvre*. For Orwell content and style are easily separated. (A very clear example of this critical assumption is to be found in the essay on Dickens where the comments on Dickens's style and technique are set off in an isolated and parenthetical section of the essay.) The modern belief in the indissoluble fusion of language and meaning formulated by such otherwise different critics as A. R. Orage, Middleton Murry and F. R. Leavis has no place in Orwell's criticism. For him a work of literature is something that can be reduced to a simple statement of outlook and something which is valuable in so far as it may serve as an objectification of his own outlook.

To the modern student of literature, Orwell's criticism must seem crude and rudimentary. Indeed, Orwell's essays about literature bear very little relationship to literary criticism as that term is now understood. Modern literary criticism, for the most part academic in origin, tends to concentrate upon given texts. Above all it is attentive to the words on the page and to the quality of mind and responsiveness to which the words attest. It is conducted by means of a set of verbal conventions that make for the neutralisation, sometimes even for the virtual extinction, of the personality of the critic. It is meticulous in its formulations even at the risk of becoming Alexandrian. With Orwell it is quite otherwise. There is no great reverence for the novel or poem as a thing in itself, nor is there much critical vocabulary. His essays seldom offer a new insight into a work. "Politics vs. Literature", for instance, though it is of great interest in term of Orwell's development and shows among other things the influence of Swift upon the writing of *Nineteen Eighty-Four*, has little to offer the reader who is primarily interested in *Gulliver's Travels*. Compared to the subtleties and complexities of recent published discussion of that book, Orwell's comments strike us as elementary. His critical essays are also often based upon reading that is casual and unreflecting. Indeed on occasion the reader can be staggered by the paucity of understanding. Orwell writes of *King Lear*, for example, "Tolstoy is right in saying that *Lear* is not a very good play as a play. It is too drawn out and has too many characters and sub-plots. One wicked daughter would have been quite enough, and Edgar is a superfluous character; indeed it would probably be a better play if Gloucester and both his sons were eliminated."[61] This is without a doubt the worst example of Orwell's lack of critical sophistication. But it serves to pinpoint the failure in critical rigorousness which manifests itself, though much less sensationally, in much of his criticism.

These deficiencies are also accompanied by, perhaps in part they may be explained by, Orwell's inability to recognise any real function or value in the practice of literary criticism. The essays abound with passages that express his confusion and irritation about the whole undertaking: "As a rule, an aesthetic preference is either something inexplicable or it is so corrupted by non-aesthetic motives as to make one wonder whether the whole of literary criticism is not a huge network of humbug." ("Charles Dickens") "Nor, is there any way of definitely proving that—for instance—Warwick Deeping is 'bad'. Ultimately there is no test of literary merit except survival, which is itself an index to majority opinion." ("Lear, Tolstoy and the Fool") "I often have the feeling that even at the best of times literary criticism is fraudulent, since in the absence of any accepted standards whatever—any *external* references which can give meaning to the statement that such and such a book is 'good' or 'bad'—every literary judgment consists in trumping up a set of rules to justify an instinctive preference." ("Writers and Leviathan") Now when we recall the rapid developments in literary criticism in Orwell's own lifetime (the lifespan of *Scrutiny*[62] was pretty well coextensive with Orwell's career as a writer), these comments strike us all the more forcibly as those of an untutored amateur. The methods and criteria for making value judgments as proposed in that periodical together with the propositions as to the value of the educated sensibility and the importance of the common pursuit do not appear to have affected Orwell's criticism at all. It seems very strange that in a period in which the practice of literary criticism was so vital and

[61] For some further comments on Orwell's criticism of *King Lear*, see John Wain in *Essays on Literature and Ideas*.

[62] That Orwell was to some extent familiar with *Scrutiny* is suggested by his reference to it in *Keep the Aspidistra Flying*.

refined Orwell should find himself fumbling blindly with such basic problems.

There are then, let it be said, no claims to be made for Orwell as a literary critic. However, to insist on seeing these essays as literary criticism is to misunderstand a great part of their intention. It is worth noting that the collection of essays which Orwell himself assembled under the title *Critical Essays* has for its subtitle "Studies in Popular Culture". The subtitle makes a very important emphasis. For it is not so much literary criticism that we are offered as discussion of a particular social area of English culture. It is a culture in which books are important, but one which also finds expression in, say, boys' comics and seaside comic postcards. It is the culture of the lower middle class and also, more significantly for Orwell, the culture of the literate working class, the class to which he had so long sought access. And these essays are interesting as a record of Orwell's continuing attempt to achieve through books what he had been unable to achieve in actuality, namely a closer and more intimate contact with and understanding of the life of "the common people". One reason that he is led to examine and to write about boys' comics and the magazines to be found in any small newsagent's shop is that "probably the contents of these shops is the best available indication of what the mass of the people thinks." The postcards of Donald McGill also afford much insight into proletarian life. For instance, the postcard convention that "there is the 'spooning' couple and the middle-aged, cat-and-dog couple, but nothing in between" is seen as reflecting "on a comic level, the working-class outlook which takes it as a matter of course that youth and adventure—almost, indeed, individual life—end with marriage". "And in this," Orwell adds, "as usual, they are more traditional, more in accord with the Christian past than the well-to-do women who try to stay young at forty by means of physical jerks, cosmetics and avoidance of childbearing." Even an avowedly literary essay such as the one on Charles Dickens is inspired by the same motives. Orwell admires Dickens in part because Dickens "is able to reach simple people", and because of his ability to express "in a comic, simplified and therefore memorable form the native decency of the common man". Orwell's studies in popular culture are to be regarded then as one way in which he continues to pursue acquaintance with what he conceives to be humane, or to use his own word, decent. What was sought after in the thirties in direct experience is in the forties searched out in books. *Critical Essays* draws attention to a set of cultural artifacts in which powerful and, for Orwell, regenerative feeling is to be found.

This very personal interest in popular culture is not the only theme of *Critical Essays*. Another and equally extra-literary preoccupation (it is to be found in virtually every essay in the collection) is with the history of this culture and the changes that have taken place within it, and indeed within English life as a whole, since the years immediately prior to the first World War. These changes are felt and represented by Orwell as part of his own personal experience, as an aspect of the painful disjunction between the worlds of childhood and adulthood. An interesting example of his treatment of this theme is the essay "Wells, Hitler and the World State". It shows very clearly how an ostensibly literary subject is subordinated to a fundamentally historical and autobiographical concern. In the first paragraph Orwell rapidly exposes Wells's false estimate of the military power of the Nazis in 1941. Then he proceeds to consider why Wells was capable of such an unrealistic view and concludes that Wells was blinded and deluded by his faith in science, progress and reason. For Orwell, forces other than these have determined the direction of recent history, forces whose power Wells was unable or unwilling to recognise. "The energy that actually shapes the world springs from emotions—racial pride, leader-worship, religious belief, love of war—which liberal intellectuals write off as anachronisms, and which they have usually destroyed so completely in themselves as to have lost all power of action." Towards the middle of the essay Orwell's gathering dissatisfaction with Wells expresses itself in a rather heavyhanded way. "He has an invincible hatred of the fighting, hunting, swashbuckling side of life, symbolised in all his early books by a violent propaganda against horses." But in the last three paragraphs the scorn suddenly abates and Orwell's tone changes. The criticism of Wells is suddenly halted by the question: "But is it not a sort of parricide for a person of my age (thirty-eight) to find fault with H. G. Wells?" Then follows a long and affectionate account of what Wells had meant to him in early life. "Thinking people who were born about the beginning of this century are in some sense Wells's own creation. . . . I doubt whether anyone who was writing books between 1900 and 1920 influenced the young so much." So clearly the present inadequacy in outlook of the man who was the "inspired prophet of the Edwardian age" is also the inadequacy of Orwell's own youthful outlook. The polemical manner of the early part of the essay has now given way to regretful reminiscence. And come the last paragraph, it is not so much Wells who is unsatisfactory as the contemporary world. "Wells is too sane to understand the modern world." Thus the over-all effect is again one of blatant contradiction. Wells is criticised because his beliefs are superannuated. And yet at the same time these beliefs are recognised as sane and proper. Orwell depreciates Wells, yet he cannot withhold admiration for him.

Implicit in this essay is another contradiction. Churchill is invoked as an antidote to Wellsian illusions, and so is Kipling. "If one had to choose among Wells's own contemporaries a writer who could stand towards him as a corrective, one might choose Kipling, who was not deaf to the evil voices of power and military glory." It is by no means clear what Orwell means by "stand towards him as a corrective". To what extent is Orwell accepting Kipling's views? How can we, as Orwell seems to suggest we should, relate Kipling's outlook to Wells whom Orwell regards as, like Dickens, "a nineteenth-century Liberal"? The obscurity here is not to be lessened by consulting Orwell's essay on Kipling. For this essay in criticism, which is also an essay in cultural history and autobiography, is one of his most tentative and inconclusive. Kipling, we find, affords Orwell some release in his frustration with the complexities of liberal motives and outlook: 'A humanitarian is always a hypocrite, and Kipling's understanding of this is perhaps the central secret of his power to create telling phrases." But then of what value is a writer of whom one must say, as Orwell does, "It is no use pretending that Kipling's view of life, as a whole, can be accepted or even forgiven by any civilised person"? The dilemma that is here objectified in the confrontation of Wells and Kipling is one of the major issues of Orwell's experience in the forties and one which is by no means restricted to the essays on literature. The events of this decade deeply disturbed any confidence Orwell may have had in liberal, progressive principles, those principles defined by, say, Fielding in E. M. Forster's *Passage to India* as "culture, good-will and intelligence". But though Orwell could criticise confidently the liberal intellect and its inadequacies, he found it hard to be articulate about the emotional drives which he regarded as the more telling in human affairs. This is a very complex and important issue and one to which I shall return when I come to consider the essays in current autobiography. For the moment I merely wish to emphasise the way in which Edwardian writers such as Wells and Kipling serve Orwell as reference points in interpreting his own history and also, for he sees them as bound together, the history of modern times.

The Edwardian reference is one that is employed over and over again in *Critical Essays*. One of the things that fascinates Orwell in boys' weeklies, for example, is the change that has taken place in them since that time. "The world of the *Skipper* and the *Champion* is still the pre-1914 world of the *Magnet* and the *Gem*." Nevertheless, in them as in the world generally there has emerged "bully-worship and the cult of violence". "Raffles and Miss Blandish" deals with the same thing: "*No Orchids* is the 1939 version of glamourised crime, *Raffles* the 1900 version." "What I am concerned with here," Orwell writes, "is the immense difference in moral atmosphere between the two books, and the changes in the popular attitude that this probably implies." While he continually defines and documents this all important change, Orwell is also engaged by those who, like H. G. Wells, try to live in the modern world with an outlook formed in the years before the change took place. So many of the figures about whom Orwell chooses to write fall into this category. P. G. Wodehouse, to whom he devotes a whole essay, is perhaps the best example. Orwell's initial motive in writing about him (and this is often the case) is polemical. His purpose is to defend Wodehouse against those who either ignorantly or unscrupulously called him a Fascist, not only on the basis of his broadcasts from Nazi Germany but also on the evidence of his novels. Orwell has no hesitation in proposing the defence:

". . . I have followed his work fairly closely since 1911, when I was eight years old, and am well acquainted with its peculiar mental atmosphere. . . ." "It is nonsense to talk of 'fascist tendencies' in his books. There are no post-1918 tendencies at all." Orwell also defends Kipling against the same charge: "Kipling's outlook is pre-Fascist. He still believes that pride comes before a fall and that the gods punish *hubris*. He does not foresee the tank, the bombing plane, the radio and the secret police, or their psychological results." "Kipling belongs very definitely to the period 1885–1902." But Orwell does not point out pre-first World War attitudes merely in those needing his defence; he discerns the same in other modern figures as diverse as Gandhi and Salvador Dali. Orwell suggests that Gandhi's success was in great part attributable to the fact that the British government with which he had to deal was not a Fascist one; it permitted Gandhi to enjoy the publicity which was largely responsible for his success. ". . . Gandhi, who after all was born in 1869, did not understand the nature of totalitarianism. . . ." Like H. G. Wells, he is for Orwell a figure who can be admired, but whose views are rendered in great part obsolete by the advent of the totalitarian period. In his essay on Salvador Dali, Orwell also manages to detect an Edwardian element in this ostentatiously "modern" figure. "Some of Dali's drawings are reminiscent of Dürer; one seems to show the influence of Beardsley, another seems to borrow something from Blake. But the most persistent strain is the Edwardian one. . . . Take away the skulls, ants, lobsters, telephones and other paraphernalia, and every now and again you are back in the world of Barrie, Rackham, Dunsany and *Where the Rainbow Ends*." Orwell concludes that "Perhaps these things are . . . there . . . because it is to that period and that style of drawing that he really belongs."

As we continue to encounter such passages, we come more and more to suspect that the anachronistic in the outlook of these figures engages Orwell because he discerns the very same thing in himself. He too was formed intellectually as an Edwardian, but must live his life in a later time when Edwardian assumptions no longer continued serviceable. This is one of the several preoccupations in *Critical Essays* that lead us to think of that volume as a set of essays in self-understanding rather than criticism. Both the subjects that Orwell chooses to write about and his method of approaching them show a more urgent concern with the self than with art. What we think of as his literary criticism is really but a means of resolving some of the issues that are treated differently in other parts of the autobiography. The criticism also treats, in its own way, a major new issue in Orwell's life during the forties: the terrible sense of unreality that comes upon him when the totalitarian world of his adulthood completely superannuates that Edwardian world which, despite the unpleasant features described in "Such, Such Were the Joys", is his criterion of the proper life.

But before I leave the criticism, I want to mention two important ways in which these essays signify Orwell's development specifically as a writer. During the thirties, as we have seen, Orwell tried unsuccessfully to write novels in accordance with the influential symbolist aesthetic. In the literary essays of the forties, however, we see him coming to a conscious realisation of the Edwardians as his true masters. And when in *Animal Farm* and *Nineteen Eighty-Four* he eventually returns to the writing of fiction, it is to recognisably Edwardian forms that he resorts. The result is that Orwell is more successful as a novelist than ever before. The second important feature of his development suggested by these essays is the effect upon him as a writer of his unceasing effort to get close to the life of the working class. The fact that in them the contact is vicarious, maintained only at a distance by examining the comics and postcards, shows that Orwell was still unable to break through the Chinese screen he had encountered in *The Road to Wigan Pier*. As Raymond Williams remarks, "His principal failure was inevitable: he observed what was evident, the external factors, and only guessed at what was not evident, the inherent patterns of feeling."[63] Nevertheless, Orwell's pursuit of acquaintance with proletarian life, as we see from the essays in criticism, continued through the 'forties and was by no means unproductive. Above all, it conditioned his style, his manner of using the English language. Orwell's style is his particular achievement, and whatever

[63] Raymond Williams, *Culture and Society*, Anchor Books (New York, 1962) p. 312.

strength and effectiveness it has derives from the infusion into the middle-class manner of some of the forthrightness of common speech. It is by far the most important product of Orwell's excursions into working-class life and of his studies in popular culture.

I should like now to offer some comments on Orwellian style, not only because they are a necessary preface to the essays in current autobiography but also because in his style we may most clearly observe both the qualities and the deficiencies of his mind. The feature of Orwell's writing that is most often mentioned is its clarity, its lucidity. Though to stress this quality is to invite the retort that it derives from too great a simplicity in, or oversimplification of, his subject matter. John Wain has partially disposed of this objection in one of his essays on Orwell where he remarks that "He had a relatively simple subject matter to express, it is true, and his famous clarity may be admitted to arise partly from that fact; but after all, the great majority of people who write have no very complex subject matter, and one rarely finds clarity and forthrightness that would pass the Orwellian test."[64] However, to say that Orwell writes better than most writers dealing with simple subject matter, true though it may be, still does not tackle the basic objection, which I think must be allowed to stand. Especially in passages that purport to develop a logical argument, Orwell is capable of wilfully oversimplifying issues, and the fluency of his writing is often achieved at the expense of responsible investigation into the question at hand. He also has a penchant for the sweeping and often crudely abusive generalisation; we have encountered some of the worst examples in the latter part of *The Road to Wigan Pier*. Nevertheless it would be untrue to say that Orwell's lucidity always derives from such irresponsibility. In fact, only rarely is this the case. For the most part it arises from one of the most praiseworthy features of Orwell's mind, his determination to cut through the pretentious, the sham and the jargon-ridden. "The great enemy of clear language is insincerity. When there

[64] Wain, *Essays on Literature and Ideas*, p. 187.

is a gap between one's real and one's declared aims, one turns as it were instinctively to long words and exhausted idioms, like a cuttlefish squirting out ink." These words from the essay "Politics and the English Language" explain very precisely the motives behind the purposive simplicity of Orwell's style. His method is always to try to set forth the simple facts of a situation or the simple facts of his own personal responses and understanding of it. And because of this, Orwell's quest for self-knowledge, a quest conducted predominantly in social, political and literary terms, still has freshness and a life to it that more "informed" books on society, literature and politics written in his time and since do not have.

But Orwell's lucidity involves something more than his attitude to his subject. It is also a matter of tone, a sense of audience. Now one cannot say that Orwell wrote for the working class. The magazines and periodicals with which he was first associated, *The Adelphi*, *The New English Weekly* and *Horizon*, all formed part of what, for the purposes of making a distinction, we must call the "intellectual" segment of English literary culture. And although from 1942 on he wrote a weekly column "I Write as I Please" in *Tribune*, a paper that has circulation among working-class socialists, his best essays did not appear there. Nevertheless, I think it can be said that Orwell wrote as one who felt himself in touch with the working class. Above all, the tonal features of his prose suggest a middle-class writer who is trying to write as and for the working man. One of the things that makes for the simplicity of Orwell's writing is a didacticism that reminds us of other socialist teachers such as Shaw and Wells. There are the verbal gestures of the courteous schoolmaster, such as "Please notice . . ." and "Here you observe . . .". The rhetorical question is often the means of moving from one stage of an argument to the next: "Do I mean by this that England is a genuine democracy? No, not even a reader of the *Daily Telegraph* could quite swallow that." And the development of an argument is always explained to us: "It is therefore of the deepest importance to try and determine what England *is*, before guessing what part England *can play* in the huge events that are happening." Furthermore, as Richard J. Voorhees has observed, Orwell "used all the techniques of the textbook—

numbered lists, italics for particularly significant passages, headings in a variety of types, etc". But in Orwell's writing we find something that is less prominent in Wells's tutoring prose and scarcely there at all in Shaw's. And that is some verbal sense of the working class. Orwell's style suggests that though he writes to teach the working class, he has himself learned something from it. This is one reason that the didactic element in Orwell's writing never gives the impression of "talking down".

Orwell had a good ear for manners of speech. Here, for instance, is his reproduction of the language of some cockney street photographers in *Down and Out in Paris and London*:

> "There y'are, sir, took yer photo lovely. That'll be a bob."
> "But I never asked you to take it," protests the victim.
> "What, you didn't want it took? Why, we thought you signalled with your 'and. Well, there's a plate wasted! That's cost us sixpence, that 'as."

The effect upon Orwell's style of this sort of attention to the speech of the lower classes is a certain colloquial robustness. Here is an example of his normal way of writing: ". . . few people are able to imagine the radio being used for the dissemination of anything except tripe. People listen to the stuff that does actually dribble from the loudspeakers of the world and conclude that it is for that and nothing else that the wireless exists." In this passage the word "dissemination" and a construction such as that introduced by the word "conclude" establish the educated writer. But the use of the words "tripe", "stuff" and "dribble" foreshortens any aloofness from subject or readership and presents us with a felt response. It is a response whose quality, it is true, may be questioned. There is here something of that bar-room pundit attitude which we encounter from time to time in Orwell. But there is also something more valuable than mere pompous griping. The word "people", for instance, as it is used here and as it is coloured by the context, expresses a sympathetic association on Orwell's part with those who must also feel insulted by what is referred to as "tripe". The language of this sentence as a whole has a characteristically Orwellian tone, a working-class contempt for the fake and the pretentious and also a suggestion of camaraderie in the resigned acceptance of its presence.

Many of the generalisations that occur in Orwell's prose are founded upon this sense of a community of feeling united by resignation. In the essay "Lear, Tolstoy and the Fool" he writes, "Most people get a fair amount of fun out of their lives, but on balance life is suffering, and only the very young or very foolish imagine otherwise." Within its context this sentence has an arresting quality which isolated quotation cannot reproduce. Nevertheless certain of its qualities can still be appreciated: the slow resigned cadence, the Brechtian undeludedness, the compassion. These are, of course, some of the qualities Orwell most admired in the working class, qualities which he could not find in his native milieu and which required the borrowing of something of the working-class idiom for their expression. There is also now and then in Orwell's prose something of working-class humour. Here is a sentence taken from Orwell's paraphrase of Gandhi's philosophy. "There must", he says, "be some limit to what we will do in order to remain alive, and the limit is well on this side of chicken broth." There is something very North Country about this last clause. A similar quality adheres to many of Orwell's similes and metaphors. In "The Lion and the Unicorn" Orwell's comment on Sir Oswald Mosley is "He was as hollow as a jug." This simile has the same social and geographical origins as the most famous of its type, "daft as a brush". Other Orwellian similes remind us of the homely and usually uninspiring realities of English life. Modern prose, we are told, consists "less and less of *words* chosen for the sake of their meaning, and more and more of *phrases* tacked together like sections of a prefabricated hen-house." A writer can be choked by an accumulation of stale phrases, "like tea leaves blocking a sink".

These, then, are some of the proletarian features that give life and immediacy to Orwell's prose. Yet despite such assimilation, his writing also testifies to his origins and education. Though he can use the language in a way that reminds us of Bozo in *Down and Out in Paris and London*, he also uses it in a way that reminds us that he was at Eton during the 1910s. "Hard cheese, old chap!" is his comment in "Inside the Whale" on one of Housman's pessimistic verses. And though such a phrase is a caricature of this way with the language, it nevertheless recalls features of his writing to which we have already alluded in our discussion of "Shooting an Elephant" and which can be observed in most of his essays. Of the several other ways in which Orwell's style shows his early social affiliations, none is more interesting than his use of metaphor. One of the most obvious developments in educated prose style during the thirties was the exploitation of simile and metaphor as devices for reductive humour. Among Orwell's contemporaries, his friend and one-time editor Cyril Connolly was the most dedicated exponent of this device. Here, for instance, is Connolly's view of Wyndham Lewis as a writer: "He is like a maddened elephant which, careering through a village, sometimes leans against a house and carelessly demolishes the most compact masonry, trumpeting defiance to the inhabitants within, sometimes pursues a dog or a chicken or stops to uproot a shrub or bang a piece of corrugated iron."[65] And here by way of comparison are some examples of Orwell's use of the same device: ". . . after his long fast, the toad has a very spiritual look, like a strict Anglo-Catholic towards the end of Lent." James Burnham is said to regard humanity as being divided into two classes: "the self-seeking hypocritical minority, and the brainless mob whose destiny is always to be led or driven, as one gets a pig back to the sty by kicking it on the bottom or by rattling a stick inside a swill bucket according to the needs of the moment." This device has, of course, become all too familiar to us since Orwell's time. It is part of the stock in trade not only of, say, John Osborne, but also of many journalists. It is one of the ways in which the time has expressed its irreverence and its disgust. Nevertheless, if this item of Orwell's style is part of a general and continuing tendency, it is clear that he has employed it in a very personal way. If we compare the similes from Orwell's writing quoted above with that from Cyril Connolly, we may see how the same device may serve two very different authorial purposes. Connolly's simile is carefully developed and obviously enjoyed by its author as much for its own sake as for the damage intended to Wyndham Lewis. With

[65] Cyril Connolly, *Enemies of Promise*, Penguin Books (London, 1958), p. 73.

the Orwell similes it is otherwise. They are less managed, more blunt; they obviously serve as a means of releasing pent-up anger and disgust in the writer. Orwell, we see, may have shared the manner of his contemporaries, but the feeling behind the manner is different. It is much stronger and more dynamic.

But to conclude a discussion of Orwell's style with a simple affirmation of its life and vitality is not possible. For we must also take account of the obvious fact that it is often unrefined, unmediated by sufficient intellect. In one way this is a simple but necessary judgement on Orwell's talent. His mind, few would deny, was not of the greatest distinction. Nevertheless I think there is something more to be said about this deficiency in his writing. And it is something which brings us very close to the major theme of the essays in current autobiography, namely his contempt for and his utter rejection of the intellectual life of his time. As we read through these essays we see that their most recurrent theme is Orwell's anger with the intellectual commu- nity—a community which he could neither participate in nor respect. And this repudiation involves matters of style as well as of attitude. In this regard, I think it is revealing that his vocabu- lary should be so conspicuously lacking in the terminology fashionable among intellectuals in the thirties and forties. It is noteworthy, for instance, that an essay in self-analysis like "Such, Such Were the Joys", an essay with such obviously Freudian implications, employs no Freudian terms. Also striking is the fact that Orwell, given as he is to interpret his experience in social, political and historical terms rarely uses any of the voca- bulary of Marxism; the dialectic, we remember, he dismissed as "the pea and thimble trick". This eschewing of the fashionable jargon of intellectuals is one source of the strength of Orwell's prose. But it is also apparent that his repudiation of and his severance from the contemporary intellectual community seriously damaged his writing. His prose suffers greatly from being deprived of the effect of the interplay of critical intelli- gence which such a community exists to provide.

A deeper understanding of the reasons for Orwell's estrange- ment from the intellectual life of his time will emerge from a consideration of the third and final group of his essays, the group which I have proposed calling essays in current autobiography. To this group I now want to turn. The category is, of course, flexible. For if I define it as comprising those essays which give us an account of Orwell's development during the forties, I must immediately concede that both the critical essays and the orthodox autobiographical essays have much to contribute to such an account. Nevertheless, there are special features in these two groups which make it useful to look at them separately. Furthermore, it is in the remaining essays, the essays that do not readily come under either of these headings that we may perceive most clearly Orwell's development during the last ten years of his life. If we start with the essay "Marrakech", which is just a set of impressions of the North Africa that Orwell saw during his holiday there in the summer of 1939, and continue to read through those of his essays prompted by specific experiences, incidents and occasions until we come to such essays as "Reflections on Gandhi" and "Writers and Leviathan", written at the end of his life, a very distinct and continuous picture of Orwell's intellectual history emerges. But such exhaustive attention would scarcely be justified here. It will be sufficient to consider just a few of the pieces that are good essays in their own right. Those I shall concentrate upon most are "Inside the Whale", "England your England" and "Benefit of Clergy", for these subsume all the important issues treated, usually more superficially, in essays of less intrinsic value and, when taken in chronological order, reveal very clearly the major developments in Orwell's mind and experience.

Our discussion of the second half of Orwell's autobiography must begin by returning to the point at which we temporarily abandoned it at the end of the preceding chapter, that is to say at the time of his hasty departure from Spain. The first two essays that he wrote after his return to England were "Boys' Weeklies" and "Charles Dickens". Both these essays are about "decency", that quality in human life which Orwell had experienced and so greatly admired during his time in Spain. (The Dickens essay shows in other ways how much Orwell's Spanish experiences were still with him; for instance, he is quick

127

to admire Dickens's grasp in *A Tale of Two Cities* of "the nightmare insecurity of a revolutionary period", something which "would apply pretty accurately to several countries today".) The first essay to give evidence of new concerns is the very next one that he wrote, "Inside the Whale". This is a famous essay in its own right; it is also one of the most important documents of Orwell's autobiography. At first sight it might seem to belong with the essays in literary criticism, for its most ostensible subject is Henry Miller's novel *Tropic of Cancer*. The first section is an appreciation of Miller's book both in itself and as a symptom of a new phase in English literary history; the second section offers an account of this history from the time of the first World War, and the final section returns to Miller, emphasising (and also commending) his "passive" novels as a departure from the propagandist literature of the thirties. And certainly the essay is interesting as literary comment. The second section, in particular, is of considerable significance as a description of twentieth-century English letters viewed from the standpoint of 1940, even though as literary history it is both highly selective and prone to journalistic simplifications. ("The wind was blowing from Europe, and long before 1930 it had blown the beer-and-cricket school naked, except for their knighthoods.") Nevertheless, the most vital issue of "Inside the Whale" is not primarily one of literary criticism. Rather it is the appearance of a totally new impulse in Orwell's mind, an impulse of quietism and despair. Henry Miller, it turns out, has more than literary significance for Orwell. He is remembered as someone who represents a radical and not easily answered challenge to Orwell's previous values and beliefs. The following sentences more than any others define the experience that lies at the very heart of the essay:

> I first met Miller at the end of 1936, when I was passing through Paris on my way to Spain. What most intrigued me about him was to find that he felt no interest in the Spanish war whatsoever. He merely told me that to go to Spain at that moment was the act of an idiot. He could understand anyone going there for purely selfish motives, out of curiosity, for instance, but to mix oneself up in such things *from a sense of obligation* was sheer stupidity. In any case my ideas about combating Fascism, defending democracy,

etc., etc., were all baloney. Our civilisation was destined to be swept away and replaced by something so different that we should scarcely regard it as human—a prospect that did not bother him, he said.

There are two noteworthy points in this very important autobiographical fragment. The first is that Orwell, even before he arrived in Spain, was thinking in terms of "combating Fascism" and "defending democracy". This would seem to contradict his statement in the opening pages of *Homage to Catalonia* that his joining the P.O.U.M. militia was unpremeditated, that he did it on the spur of the moment, because it seemed "the only thing to do". In the light of the remarks in "Inside the Whale" we must suspect that in *Homage to Catalonia* Orwell's reticence led him to try to camouflage his hunger for confirming experience just as it had, in a different way, in *Down and Out in Paris and London*. This is but one example of how Orwell's autobiographical writings taken as a whole and as a continuity can illuminate the individual components. The second and more important point is that the Orwell who ignored Miller's objections in 1936 and proceeded to Spain should in 1940 be returning to them in his mind. It is also worth noting that Miller's *Tropic of Cancer*, the ostensible subject of the essay, was not in 1940 a current novel. It was first published in 1935, which suggests that Orwell's attention to it was not prompted by the demands of journalism, but by his own personal interest. The fact is that Orwell now feels compelled to reconsider a writer whose attitudes four years earlier he had rejected. And it is a favourable reconsideration, one which involves a denial, or at least a radical questioning, of Orwell's own previous outlook and feelings.

In the essay Orwell has much to say about *Tropic of Cancer*; but it is not upon Miller's novels that Orwell's most vital interest centres. The crucial document (from which incidentally Orwell takes the title of his own essay) is one of Miller's discursive pieces, an essay on the diaries of Anaïs Nin. Miller compares Miss Nin as a writer to Jonah in the belly of the whale. By this comparison he intends to define, says Orwell, "the final, unsurpassable stage of irresponsibility". Furthermore, "there is no question that Miller himself is inside the whale." "All his best and most characteristic passages are written from the angle of

Jonah, a willing Jonah." "I should say that he believes in the impending ruin of Western Civilisation much more firmly than the majority of 'revolutionary writers'; only he does not feel called upon to do anything about it." And this, it turns out, is the very attitude that Orwell himself now endorses. To anyone who has followed Orwell's career through the thirties, this must seem astonishing. Nevertheless his words are quite unambiguous. "At this date it hardly even needs a war to bring home to us the disintegration of our society and the increasing helplessness of all decent people. It is for this reason that I think that the passive non-co-operative attitude implied in Miller's work is justified."

Looking, as we must, for some explanation of this sudden change in outlook, we may discover several possible causes. First there is the "helplessness of all decent people". By now Franco was victorious in Spain and the cause which had been of such great importance to Orwell personally was irretrievably lost. Then there is the second World War, which broke out while Orwell was actually writing this essay. In the words which I cited above, this is conceded as a reason, though an extra and a superfluous one, for accepting the fact of "helplessness". Finally, and this emerges most forcefully in terms of the essay as a whole, there is Orwell's bitter dissatisfaction with the left-wing intelligentsia and its prescriptions. With the defeat of the Spanish loyalists, the public-spiritedness of the left, its world-historical and politically prescriptive manner of responding to events becomes, in Orwell's view, just so much redundant verbiage. Even while he was actually in Spain, left-wing rhetoric about the war had seemed to him a denial, often vicious and purposeful, of the true and human actuality. But by 1940 he also sees this rhetoric as a testimony to the unrealism on the part of the articulate and influential left that makes possible the continuing aggression of an atavistic Fascism. And this is why Orwell commends the determinedly personal and honest and "irresponsible" outlook of a Henry Miller; it is one way of attacking the public vision of socialist writers, which for Orwell is not only inaccurate and unviable, but dangerous.

Orwell continues to return to this attack throughout the remainder of his life. There is scarcely a major essay in which he does not, in one way or another, resume it. And, of course, this concern lies at the very heart of his last novel, *Nineteen Eighty-Four*. "Inside the Whale", taken in its proper context, is not the exclusively literary essay that it may appear to be when read in isolation. It is the first chapter in a new phase of Orwell's autobiography. It is his first sustained criticism of the quality of the intellectual life of his time and also his first essay in defining the proper function of the intellectual. We see, for instance, that the second section of the essay is there not primarily as a piece of dispassionate literary history, but rather as a polemic against the "thirties" movement. This section is organised around two questions: What is communism? And why were the young English writers of the thirties attracted to it? The first is answered quickly and contemptuously: "The communist movement in Western Europe began as a movement for the violent overthrow of capitalism, and degenerated within a few years into an instrument of Russian foreign policy." The second question is dealt with more carefully and at greater length. Orwell suggests that communism was a faith for a generation that had lost faith in (and Orwell seems to understand this loss) "Patriotism, religion, the Empire, the family, the sanctity of marriage, the Old School Tie, birth, breeding, honour, discipline . . . .". A further reason offered is "the softness and serenity of life in England itself". And here we come upon the nub of Orwell's objections to the intellectual left, his feeling that it is unacquainted with reality. "So much of left-wing thought," he maintains, "is a kind of playing with fire by people who don't even know that fire is hot." His well-known criticism of two stanzas from W. H. Auden's *Spain 1937* is reinforced immediately by a reference to his own first-hand experience. "Personally I would not speak so lightly of murder. It so happens that I have seen the bodies of numbers of murdered men—I don't mean killed in battle, I mean murdered. Therefore I have some conception of what murder means—the terror, the hatred, the howling relatives, the post-mortems, the blood, the smells. To me, murder is something to be avoided. So it is to any ordinary person." Cited in isolation these words may seem pompous in a way that they do not in context. But they are a good example of Orwell's manner of scrutiny, of his habit of testing the truth of a piece of writing against his own actual experience. And they exemplify his characteristic scorn of an intellectual community which is prone to ignore the reality that is known and felt and to become enmeshed in, and excited by, mere words. A further— indeed the most radical—criticism that Orwell levels against his intellectual contemporaries involves the way in which a progressive sounding vocabulary can mask gross and barbaric motives. Once again the reference point is the all-important experience, Spain. "The thing that, to me, was truly frightening about the war in Spain was not such violence as I witnessed, nor even the party feuds behind the lines, but the immediate reappearance in left-wing circles of the mental atmosphere of the Great War. The very people who for twenty years had sniggered over their own superiority to war hysteria were the very ones who rushed straight back into the mental slum of 1915."

The power of these criticisms of the thirties left has often been admitted, even if only to be depreciated. E. P. Thompson for instance, in a retort published some twenty years later entitled "Outside the Whale", maintains that "It was in this essay more than any other that the aspirations of a generation were buried; not only was a political movement which embodied much that was honourable buried but so also was the notion of disinterested dedication to a political cause."[66] In a footnote Thompson modifies this somewhat when he writes, "It was not the only essay (Koestler's "The Yogi and the Commissar" was of equal importance) nor was its effect immediate; but the disenchanted of 1945–49 returned to the positions which Orwell had already prepared." Nevertheless, the effect which Thompson ascribes to this one essay is considerable. Since it is hardly possible to measure accurately the effect of any work of literature, one cannot easily agree or disagree with these assertions. Though one feels that however influential this particular essay may have been, it cannot on its own, or even with the support of Koestler's essay, have accomplished all that Thompson claims that it did. The exhaustion of thirties socialism and the dis-

[66] E. P. Thompson, "Outside the Whale" in *Out of Apathy* (London, 1960), p. 164. The point made in the first clause of the sentence quoted here is echoed by John Mander in his *The Writer and Commitment* (London, 1961).

enchantment of the post-war years are surely to be explained by more than the publication of "Inside the Whale". Nevertheless, Thompson's remarks are of interest because of the tribute they imply to the power of the essay. They are a corroboration of the point made earlier that Orwell's essays, even with their manifest limitations, still possess a vitality and a compelling power that is hard to find elsewhere in the prose of the period. Though there is no great subtlety of perceptiveness, there is a convincing sincerity in his account of the degeneration of the intellectual life.

Part of Orwell's strength, we may even say, lies in the fact that he has the courage of his own confusion. "Inside the Whale" as a whole is neither as clear nor as purposive as E. P. Thompson's remarks might lead us to think. As is so frequently the case with Orwell, the essay ends in some doubt and in-decisiveness. We find him hastily attaching a whole series of conditions and qualifications to his main judgment that Henry Miller "is the only imaginative prose writer of the slightest value who has appeared among the English speaking races for some years past." And throughout the essay there is the characteristic uneasiness about the relationship between what is regarded as a writer's "message" and his "purely literary" achievement. Even the espousal of Millerian quietism is not quite so whole-hearted as I may have suggested. For though it is true that Orwell's words express agreement with Miller's "irresponsi-bility", nevertheless their tone suggests that the agreement is given reluctantly, even desperately. Orwell is certain about his repudiation of the way in which his left-wing contemporaries were socially conscious. This we can see in the confidence and the robustness of the prose in which he writes about them. But this is not to say that he himself finds it easy to reject all forms of social consciousness and social responsibility. He asserts that he does, and yet it cannot but strike us as an assertion *malgré lui*. What we have in "Inside the Whale" is the expression of an impulse of despair, an impulse which will appear in subsequent essays but which will never consolidate into a permanent atti-tude. Orwell, as we have seen, devoted his life to searching out a form of experience which he could affirm. It turned out to be essentially social experience. In *The Road to Wigan Pier* he had supported his affirmation with political prescription. In "Inside the Whale", written after the realisation of the political futility of the major experience of his life, Orwell is for a moment ready to jettison not merely political prescriptions but the possibility of affirmation too. "Seemingly there is nothing left but quietism —robbing reality of its terrors by simply submitting to it. Get inside the whale—or rather, admit you are inside the whale (for you *are*, of course). Give yourself over to the world process, stop fighting against it or pretending that you can control it; simply accept it, endure it, record it. That seems to be the formula that any sensitive novelist is now likely to adopt." The word "endure" in this passage best emphasises the new note of pessimism that enters Orwell's life at the start of the forties. The campaign for, the affirmation of, the good life have faltered. (In this regard we remember his somewhat envious paragraphs about Walt Whitman in the essay.) And yet at the same time the passage I have quoted shows that this interpretation of the state of the world depends greatly upon semblances; words such as 'seemingly" and "seems" show that there are reservations lying behind Orwell's commitment to pessimism. And indeed, as we shall see when we look at later essays, pessimism was not to take complete possession of Orwell's life and writing. It remained a perpetual possibility, but then so also did that other more characteristic Orwellian impulse, the desire to know, proclaim and defend the experience of more abundant life.

An important concomitant of this new impulse of despair is a change in Orwell's thinking about literature and especially about the novel. It signifies, above all, a new attitude to the tradition emanating from the figure of Axel. We can see this change in Orwell's comments upon Julien Green's *Minuit*, a novel which owes much to the tradition of Edgar Allan Poe and Villiers de l'Isle-Adam. It is especially revealing to compare Orwell's remarks about this book in "Inside the Whale" in 1940 with those that he made about the same work in *The New English Weekly* of November 12th, 1936. At that time Orwell had objected to the content of Green's novel; he had attacked it for ignoring the social and political realities of contemporary life. "The truth is that ours is not an age for mysterious romances about lunatics in ruined *chateaux*, because it is not an age in which one can be unaware of contemporary reality. You can't ignore Hitler, Mussolini, unemployment, aeroplanes and the radio; you can only pretend to do so, which means lopping off a large part of your consciousness." In "Inside the Whale" Orwell still dislikes the book; but now, and this is the important thing, the criteria for judgment have changed. Orwell does not object to the lack of social concern nor to the characteristically *symboliste* subject matter. He even concedes implicitly that a work of art may properly serve to evoke a state of mind and in such a way provide an aesthetic experience. And it is in aesthetic terms that he condemns *Minuit*. "One sees the difference immediately if one compares Poe's *Tales* with what is, in my opinion, an insincere attempt to work up a similar atmosphere, Julien Green's *Minuit*. The thing that immediately strikes one about *Minuit* is that there is no reason why any of the events in it should happen. Everything is completely arbitrary; there is no emotional sequence. But this is exactly what one does *not* feel with Poe's stories. . . . Because they are true within a certain framework, they keep the rules of their own peculiar world, like a Japanese picture." Between these two very different responses to the same symbolist work there lies a new understanding of that particular type of literary art, an understanding born of the same disillusion which is expressed in different ways elsewhere in the essay. It is not too great an oversimplification, I think, to say that with the pessimism that overtook him around 1940, Orwell came to have a new sympathy for the dominant literary aesthetic of his time, a sympathy which is different from the mere imitation that characterised the novels he wrote in the thirties. That this new susceptibility to the symbolist view of experience stays with him is shown by *Nineteen Eighty-Four*, which is more genuinely a work of symbolist art than anything Orwell ever wrote. The main fact about "Inside the Whale" in terms of Orwell's autobiography is that it proposes this new manner of understanding both literature and experience.

"Inside the Whale" was written at the time of the outbreak of the second World War. Orwell's next major essay, "England Your England", was written during the London blitz. The opening single sentence paragraph establishes the situation swiftly and dramatically. "As I write, highly civilised human beings are flying overhead trying to kill me." What is most immediately interesting about this essay is that it shows how the impulse of despair present in "Inside the Whale" in no way hardened into a firm position. The chief purpose of "England Your England" is to offer optimistic and constructive suggestions about dealing with the war-time emergency. It was written originally not as a separate and independent essay but as the first chapter of the book *The Lion and the Unicorn*, which, as Christopher Hollis has remarked, "was a work of conscious war-time propaganda".[67] The two chapters that follow, "Shopkeepers at War" and "The English Revolution", develop the argument that only by means of a socialist revolution can England become rejuvenated and thus capable of winning the war against the Fascist powers. Today these chapters, with their analysis of the current political situation and the six-point socialist programme which they set forth, are of no more interest to most readers than the two forgotten essays Orwell contributed to Victor Gollancz's *The Betrayal of the Left*, which made some of the same points. They need to be mentioned merely because they explain the context of that more durable piece of writing which we know as "England Your England". Orwell's primary aim in this essay is to state and also to promote the essential unity and indivisibility of the English people. He begins by asserting the tremendous power of patriotic feeling as a force in human affairs, a power which intellectuals have failed to understand. "Christianity and international socialism are as weak as straw in comparison with it." This feeling, it is clear from the essay, was very strong in Orwell himself. But given the time at which he wrote, he could not but be aware of the evil consequences of a certain form of national feeling, and the problem of defining its proper form is one to which he continually returns. It is dealt with in such essays as "Notes on Nationalism" and "Anti-semitism in England". In the former essay Orwell defines patriotism as "devotion to a particular way of life, which one believes to be the best in the world but has no wish to force upon other people. . . ." "Patriotism is of its nature defensive, both militarily and culturally. Nationalism, on the other hand, is inseparable from the desire

[67] Hollis, p. 132.

for power. The abiding purpose of every nationalist is to secure more power and prestige, *not* for himself but for the nation or other unit in which he has chosen to sink his own individuality." It is patriotism as here defined that expresses itself in "England Your England". There is no agressiveness in either tone or content. There is no anger, for instance, against those "flying overhead trying to kill me". Orwell's interest is rather in offering some definition of that community of feeling which for him makes England what it is, "its emotional unity, the tendency of nearly all its inhabitants to feel alike and act together in moments of supreme crisis". His chief metaphors of England are those of the family and the living organism, "an everlasting animal stretching into the future and the past, and, like all living things, having the power to change out of all recognition and yet remain the same". In recent years, Orwell concedes, much has happened that threatens to disrupt this organic unity. Particularly culpable are the ruling class and the intelligentsia. In this essay, unlike the previous one, Orwell's attitude towards the intellectuals comprises more than angry criticism; it also asks for the reconciliation of the intellectual life with the national life as a whole.

The affection for England that pervades the essay attaches most strongly to Orwell's chosen images of his country, to "the clatter of clogs in the Lancashire mill towns, the to-and-fro of the lorries on the Great North Road, the queues outside the Labour exchanges, the rattle of pin tables in the Soho pubs, the old maids biking to Holy Communion through the mists of the autumn mornings . . .". Such feeling was intensified by the wartime emergency. Sometimes we feel that Orwell finds it difficult to resist complete indulgence in this particular type of emotional release. Only his innate reticence and the necessity of dealing with certain criticisms of English life hold him back. And even the rational analysis of these criticisms subserves his vision of an England that can be loved without reservation or condition, a vision that makes possible the hymnal paragraph with which the essay ends. The Orwell who in "Inside the Whale" was ready to succumb to despair now again proposes a vision of the good life. It is a vision of an England in which the common culture is paramount, an England in which the present middle class either disappears or becomes converted to the humanity of the common culture.

The failings in English life which Orwell concedes are: hypocrisy, snobbery, privilege, "the vein of political ignorance" and "the stupidity of the ruling class". Orwell regards the last as the chief source of England's present difficulties. "A family with the wrong rulers in control—that, perhaps, is as near as one can come to describing England in a phrase." The fourth section of the essay is for the most part a history of English experience from around the time of the first World War, a history which is mainly concerned to document the blunders of a ruling class that "obviously could not admit to themselves that their usefulness was at an end". This historical sketch reminds us of the one dealing with the same time span though chiefly in terms of literary history in "Inside the Whale". Each develops and explains Orwell's view of the superannuatedness of the English middle-class manner and the dangers inherent in the continuing middle-class hegemony in English life and culture. "England Your England" also shows how Orwell's dissatisfaction with contemporary intellectual life is associated with his rejection of middle-class life generally, the life of which the intelligentsia is really a part. We realise that Orwell's explicit condemnation of the intellectuals in the forties is a continuation of his implicit condemnation of the middle class as a whole in the autobiographies of the thirties. In those books Orwell rarely attempts to anatomise the middle class, but his criticism of it is clearly implied in his search for a living community elsewhere.

In the fifth section of "England Your England" he proposes a definition of the modern intellectual by relating him to his "symbolic opposite", the Blimp. To a degree this may be seen as a metaphor for wounding. (Orwell after all presents both types in terms of extreme caricature.) But it is also intended as a literal description of a crucial defect in the English middle class. "These two seemingly hostile types, symbolic opposites—the half-pay colonel with his bull neck and diminutive brain, like a dinosaur, the highbrow with his domed forehead and stalk-like neck—are mentally linked together and constantly interacting upon one another; in any case they are born to a considerable extent into the same families." The manner, the responses, the attitudes of a Blimp are now anachronistic because the situation which demanded and created them has long since disappeared. The Empire is now ruled from Whitehall, by "well meaning, over-civilised men, in dark suits and black felt hats . . .". The intellectuals are similarly redundant because they are "purely negative creatures, mere anti-Blimps". "There is little in them except the irresponsible carping of people who have never been and never expect to be in a position of power." The intellectuals (it is interesting to note Orwell's view that since T. E. Lawrence there has been "no intelligentsia that is not in some sense 'Left'") are as much out of touch with reality as the Blimps whom they oppose. They are marked by "the emotional shallowness of people who live in a world of ideas and have little contact with physical reality". On the one hand is emotion divorced from intelligence and on the other, intelligence uninformed by feeling. The result is a paralysis in proper thought and action.

Orwell's purpose does not halt at mere criticism; it also involves a plea for reconciliation between thought and feeling or in the particular terms of the essay, between "patriotism and intelligence". It is, he says, "the fact that we are fighting a war and a very peculiar kind of war, that may make this possible." (This, we may note in passing, was not merely a prescription and a hope for others but also one of the main endeavours of Orwell's own life; it is clear that he recognised both the Blimp and the intellectual within himself. In comparison with writers of other times who shared this concern Orwell's approach may seem fumbling and awkward. But we cannot think of any of his coevals who tried so urgently to relate fruitfully the intellect and common experience in both self and society.) The reconciliation between mind and feeling in English life that Orwell proposed envisioned the disappearance of the existing middle class; "the Bloomsbury highbrow, with his mechanical snigger, is as out of date as the cavalry colonel." The title of this essay is, of course, an echo of some words of W. E. Henley's, words which D. H. Lawrence also employed as the title of a story. For Orwell, as for Lawrence, the chief fact about the modern English community is the exhaustion of moral energy in the long dominant middle class. The model of a proper community, based upon a realistic view of life and upon sensible emotions, is now to be found in England only among the common people, who presently "must live to some extent *against* the existing order". The two qualities in the common people which Orwell particularly admires and which in his view differentiate them from the middle class are "their extreme gentleness" and "their deeply moral attitude to life". For Orwell these qualities must come to inform all areas of English life if any full sense of a living national community is to be regained. It is to such an enterprise that he commits himself and to which he invites others, Blimps and intellectuals alike, and also the general reader.[68] "For it is *your* civilisation, it is *you*." "Good or evil, it is yours, you belong to it, and this side of the grave you will never get away from the marks that it has given you."

The elements of exhortation and celebration to be found in "England Your England" are things of the moment: they do not recur in any of the essays that follow. We may suppose that as the national danger receded and the likelihood of a revolutionary new order diminished, Orwell felt a lessening inclination and opportunity for prophecy and turned again to his own more immediately personal concerns. As we know, during the latter years of the war he was engaged in writing *Animal Farm*. And in the essays of the same period the dominant concern is with the proper function of the literary artist. Essays such as "Rudyard Kipling", "W. B. Yeats", "Arthur Koestler" and "Benefit of Clergy" besides being reviews are essays in the framing of an aesthetic. They renew more optimistically the discussion initiated at a time of great despair in "Inside the Whale". "Benefit of

[68] Orwell, it should be noted, has some suspicion that the new classless society which he predicts and calls for may be something quite different from a society revitalised by the, to him, humane qualities of the old working class. In the new towns of the Thames Valley ("the place to look for the genius of the future England"), he sees "a civilisation in which children grow up with an intimate knowledge of magnetoes and in complete ignorance of the Bible". However, Orwell quickly averts his eyes from this particular possibility in democratic culture, remarking that "The new red cities of Greater London are crude enough but these things are only the rash that accompanies a change."

Clergy", for example, tells us much about Orwell's thinking about art in the mid-forties and has a great relevance to his practice of the art of fiction in *Animal Farm* and *Nineteen Eighty-Four*. It starts off as a review of Savador Dali's autobiography. Orwell concedes that Dali is "a draughtsman of very exceptional gifts". "He has fifty times more talent than most of the people who would denounce his morals and jeer at his paintings." Nevertheless, concerning what he calls "the moral atmosphere and mental scenery" of Dali's work, Orwell is, for once, in no doubt: "It is a book that stinks." And a considerable part of the essay is devoted to retelling the incidents in Dali's book which elicit such unqualified disgust. But Dali also raises a more general issue for Orwell, namely the relationship and the responsibility of the artist to society. And this is the important part of the essay. It reveals a new development in Orwell's mind, which becomes very clear if we place this essay beside "Inside the Whale".

Both Miller and Dali were at some time and in some phases of their work "surrealists"; certainly Orwell himself identified them as such. Nevertheless his attitude to the novelist in the earlier essay and his attitude some three years later to the painter are strikingly different. Henry Miller was commended for his attitude of indifference, of irresponsibility towards society. Dali, however, is angrily criticised for his failures as "a citizen and a human being". Dali is also reproved for expressing private fantasies; he and they, we are told, are "a symptom of the world's sickness". In Henry Miller, on the other hand, it is a matter of distinction and achievement that he has "chosen to drop the Geneva language of the ordinary novel and drag the *Realpolitik* of the inner mind into the open". It may be that for Orwell there is something to prefer in what is discovered in Miller's inner mind to that in Dali's. But the fact remains that in the later essay Orwell is in arms against a form of art which is not socially responsible in a way that he certainly was not in the earlier one. The assumptions about what art should be are quite different. Taken together these essays illustrate a divergence in Orwell's mind that is of crucial importance for understanding his own art in *Animal Farm* and *Nineteen Eighty-Four*. At one time he concedes the rightness of an art which abdicates all social responsibility and concerns itself only with private experience, feelings and responses. He is, in fact, very close to accepting those aesthetic premises which he himself termed "Art for Art's Sake". And yet it is also true that Orwell could not rest content with that position. There was always in him the propagandist, the polemicist, the crusader, the man who above all sought to see in society as a whole the qualities of feeling and relationship which he himself, as we know from his autobiographies, had known in various ways, the man who at the very end of his life could maintain that "every line of serious work that I have written since 1936 has been written, directly or indirectly, *against* totalitarianism and *for* democratic socialism. . . ." Clearly "Inside the Whale" is a notable exception to the truth of this statement. Indeed, throughout the forties, there is a deep ambivalence that he never finally resolves either theoretically in his essays or in practice in his actual fictions. For if *Animal Farm* demonstrates an adherence to the socially purposive view, *Nineteen Eighty-Four*, his most sustained and successful work of fiction, suggests something of a resumption in the late forties of the position defined in "Inside the Whale" at the beginning of the decade.

"Benefit of Clergy" was first published in 1944, that is to say around the time Orwell was completing *Animal Farm*. In the four years or so that intervene between this time and the publication of *Nineteen Eighty-Four* there are no essays that are especially interesting as individual pieces. But taken as a continuity the essays of these years show very clearly the emotional and intellectual development that is the prelude to the writing of Orwell's last major work. One of his principal concerns during these years is religion. And though in this matter as in so many others it is difficult to say confidently what his position was, there is no doubt as to the importance of the issue for him. "The major problem of our time," he says in 'Looking Back on the Spanish War', "is the decay of the belief in personal immortality." And in the essay on Arthur Koestler he remarks that "The real problem is how to restore the religious attitude while accepting death as final." The whole issue, we come to see, was for him a social rather than a theological one. Obviously Orwell himself is unable to accept the idea of life after death, and yet at the same time there is in him a longing for the sort of moral order in society which he imagined to be possible in a world of faith. Orwell's feeling of nostalgia comes out clearly in the little autobiographical poem written in 1935 which, in 1947, he thought worthwhile reprinting in the essay "Why I write":

> A happy vicar I might have been
> Two hundred years ago,
> To preach upon eternal doom
> And watch my walnuts grow;

A life of non-fanatical churchmanship lived in the countryside of Georgian England, then, is a possibility which Orwell finds attractive. This manner of intellectual life contrasts sharply with that of the modern intellectuals whose worst follies, Orwell remarks in "Notes on Nationalism", "have been made possible by the breakdown of patriotism and religious belief." Nevertheless, even though Orwell is sometimes ready to proclaim the value of religious belief, particularly as a means of sustaining his unceasing criticism of fellow intellectuals, it is indisputable that the commitment to which his essays as a whole testify is, to use his own terms, humanist rather than Christian. For though he may have cherished some idea of a Christian society, he could not approve the ideas, the state of mind and the behaviour which are considered Christian. In "Lear, Tolstoy and the Fool" he writes: "Ultimately it is the Christian attitude which is self-interested and hedonistic, since the aim is always to get away from the painful struggle of earthly life and find eternal peace in some kind of Heaven or Nirvana. The humanist attitude is that the struggle must continue and that death is the price of life." In a Christian such as Tolstoy, he believes, a particular form of power-seeking underlies religious zeal. He suspects that one of Tolstoy's motives is to enjoy a subtle type of "power over other people". "Tolstoy renounced wealth, fame and privilege; he abjured violence in all its forms and was ready to suffer for doing so; but it is not easy to believe that he abjured the principle of coercion, of at least the desire to coerce others." "For if you have embraced a creed which appears to be free from the ordinary dirtiness of politics—a creed from which you yourself cannot expect to draw any material advantage—surely that proves that you are in the right? And the more you are in the right, the more natural that everyone else should be bullied into thinking likewise." This suspicion of the motives of the religious is still in Orwell's mind when, in one of his very last essays, he reviews Gandhi's autobiography. His suspicion is capsulated in the dictum of the opening sentence: "Saints should always be judged guilty until they are proved innocent. . . ." Orwell gives the impression of being friendlier towards Gandhi than he is towards Tolstoy. However, both essays lead Orwell into a consideration of what he sees as the essential inhumanity of a lived religion. "The essence of being human," he says as though in answer to Gandhi, "is that one does not seek perfection, that one *is* sometimes willing to commit sins for the sake of loyalty, that one does not push asceticism to the point where it makes friendly intercourse impossible." In Tolstoy, too, he sees a contempt for the actual processes of life and for ordinary human relationships: "His main aim, in his later years, was to narrow the range of human consciousness." "If only, Tolstoy says in effect, we would stop breeding, fighting, struggling and enjoying, if we could get rid not only of our sins but of everything else that binds us to the surface of the earth— including love, then the whole painful process would be over and the Kingdom of Heaven would arrive." The phrase "the surface of the earth" is one which has a special significance for Orwell towards the end of his life. It recurs, for instance, in "Why I Write". "So long as I remain alive and well I shall continue to feel strongly about prose style, to love the surface of the earth, and to take a pleasure in solid objects and scraps of useless information." The phrase, it would seem, came to signify for Orwell his acceptance of the ordinary human realities of life and also his rejection of all doctrines—religious, metaphysical and aesthetic—that would seek to reduce man's awareness of them.

This concern with religion which we encounter in the last essays may in part be attributable to Orwell's own illness. But there is also, I think, another and a more important reason. For his discussions of religion, when inspected closely, turn out to be discussions of what he considered one of the most frightening tendencies in the life of his time, namely power worship, the religion of power. If he criticised Tolstoy and his religion for seeking to reduce the consciousness of men, his criticism was even more forcefully directed against those of his own time who sought to do the same thing in order to enjoy the ruthless and sadistic exercise of power. The growth of "realism", "meaning the doctrine that might is right . . . has been the great feature of the intellectual history of our own age," he remarks in "Raffles and Miss Blandish". "Why this should be so," he continues, "is a complicated question. The interconnection between sadism, masochism, success-worship, power-worship, nationalism and totalitarianism is a huge subject whose edges have barely been scratched, and even to mention it is considered somewhat indelicate." This indelicate subject is, of course, the chief theme of *Nineteen Eighty-Four*. Clearly, what we have in the last essays is a return to the same thing that during the thirties, had so deeply troubled Orwell about the class situation in England. As a result of his experiences in the North of England and in Spain he had been able to propose a humane alternative to a system of sado-masochistic relationships. But the horrors of the second World War and especially their effect on human sensibility created again a situation that challenged the Orwellian idea of proper human relationship, the idea of "friendly intercourse", just as they had also challenged his ideas of literary art. The essays that Orwell wrote towards the end of his life show him caught up in a world where "power over" is a normal desire, and where in the interests of such power there is a denial of the simple facts of reality, a falsification of history and a repudiation of human relationship.

There is a symmetry in Orwell's career. In the thirties, through a determined involvement in experience, he came to achieve an essentially democratic view of human and social relationships, of communication and of letters. The great culmination of this effort is to be found in *Homage to Catalonia*. During the forties this view is challenged. There are occasions when Orwell may be seen to have renounced it. During these years Orwell found himself passive before terrible events which he was unable fully to interpret. And though, despite strong impulses of despair, he adhered to his achieved position, this decade led him to no such happy confirmation as the thirties had done. We may put this all important distinction another way by saying that at the end of the thirties Orwell came to pay his homage to Catalonia, but that at the end of the following decade his most sustained expression of his view of experience was to be found in *Nineteen Eighty-Four*.

5

Orwell became famous with the publication of *Animal Farm* in 1945. Upon this book, together with *Nineteen Eighty-Four* and the essays, his reputation continues chiefly to rest. Today it is very difficult to share the admiration with which *Animal Farm* was received when it first appeared. All the comparisons with *Gulliver's Travels* and *Candide* that are to be found in the contemporary reviews must now seem, twenty years on, extremely damaging to Orwell's book. And only when we recall that its publication coincided with the beginning of the Cold War does its instant success become understandable. Certainly as a mocking allegory of the first thirty years or so of the Russian revolution it is a work of considerable poise, a poise that derives from Orwell's long nurtured cynicism about communism, which had resisted the indulgent attitude to Russia born of the war-time alliance as much as it had resisted the fashionable communism of literary and intellectual circles during the thirties. But for the reader of today it is this very poise which makes the book trivial. The allegory is too pat, the confidence of the narrator (the confidence of one telling a nursery tale) too secure. Orwell's "fairy story" is only a clever form for expressing a set of opinions that have been held so long that they no longer admit the complexity of the experience they claim to explain.

The story of the humanised beasts of *Animal Farm* treats of events that are in many ways similar to those in which Orwell himself had participated in Spain. As in *Homage to Catalonia*, we have an account of a revolution created by a community undergoing persecution and deprivation. But idealism and communal energy and purpose do not long endure, we are told again, and the selfish and the unscrupulous take over the revolution and recreate the same sort of class system and exploitation which the revolution had overthrown. It is a measure of the poverty of *Animal Farm* that it does little more than rehearse these "points". In *Homage to Catalonia* such conclusions were merely one part of an intense and movingly evoked experience. But in *Animal Farm* they form the totality of what the book has to offer us. We may perhaps derive some pleasure from elucidating the allegory. We may identify old Major, the aged porker who has the dream and who provides the ideological impulse to the revolution, as Karl Marx, and we may recognise the quarrel between Napoleon and Snowball as representing the rift between Stalin and Trotsky. And we may like to find the allegorical counterparts of the treason trials, the emergence of the Soviet secret police, the drive for technological achievement, the perversion of the ideals of the revolution and the misuse of propaganda.[69] Nevertheless, if there is any pleasure in making such discoveries, it is hardly a literary pleasure. Indeed, in specifically literary terms, there is only one aspect of the book that continues to interest us and that is its form, and the particular tone of voice which this form enjoins upon the author. And the form is noteworthy not because of any particular distinction which it involves for the book, but rather because it is Orwell's first renewed effort to solve the problem of form in prose fiction which had been abandoned since the writing of *Coming Up For Air*.

Animal Farm is subtitled "A Fairy Story". Since the book does not tell of fairies, nor yet of the magical, this description seems hardly appropriate. Still it does suggest one intention of the book, which is to tell a story directly and simply. In this respect Orwell's purpose is a characteristic one, namely the vigorous sweeping aside of jargon, cant and hypocrisy and the presenting of issues clearly and intelligibly. But this sort of intention always has its attendant dangers and in the telling of his fairy story Orwell has succumbed to them. His account of revolution is greatly oversimplified; it is too obvious, too facile, too easy. For whatever we may think of the Russian revolution or, for that matter of any revolution, we cannot but be aware

[69] Quite a lengthy discussion of the details of the allegory is to be found in Atkins, pp. 223–226.

that the crises of a society are much more complex than Orwell is here able to suggest. And the feelings about revolution which the book elicits are as unsophisticated as the narrative itself. Take, for instance, the emotional climax of the book which comes when Boxer, the loyal and hard-working but unintelligent work horse, emblematic of "the common people", is sold to the knackers by the pig-commissars when he becomes too ill to work any more. The feelings of simple compassion and absolutely righteous indignation which this incident is calculated to evoke may be tolerable in a nursery tale that has no pretentions to being anything other than a nursery tale. But in one which lays claim to offer the adult intelligence some feeling for the realities of modern social and political life, they cannot, because of their crudity and sentimentality, merit serious attention. At the cost of this sort of oversimplification the sustained poise of the narrative is purchased. Clearly Orwell enjoys the easy confidence to which the position of a teller of nursery tales entitles him. The avuncular security and the poker-faced humour bestowed by the conventions of the form solve completely the difficult problem of the author-reader relationship which in the past had proved so troublesome. But in order to enjoy writing in this way, Orwell has made himself oblivious of the complexity of the experience with which his story purports to deal. He has here found a form which is easy and pleasing to him, but which is a means for turning away from the disturbing complexities of experience rather than for confronting them. It allows only of simple ideas, easy responses and obvious conclusions.

This particular form of the nursery story has been borrowed from that cosy world prior to the first World War upon which, as we have seen, Orwell was so ready to dwell. *Animal Farm* especially reminds us of Kipling's stories for children. The laws of the revolution that are painted on the wall of the cowshed and chanted by the animals clearly owe something to "The Law of the Jungle" in Kipling's *Second Jungle Book*. Indeed the central device of *Animal Farm*, the convention of humanised animals, may also derive most immediately from Kipling's *Jungle Book*. And Orwell's narrative tone is obviously modelled on that of the *Just So Stories*. And of course there is the Dickensian element, that traditional element which endures beneath the experimentalism in every one of Orwell's novels and shows the strength of the premodern and the unmodern in his literary sensibility. The humour of the book, when it is not "just so" humour, is Dickensian, achieved by the use of "the unnecessary detail" which Orwell in his critical essay had identified and given examples of and relished as "the unmistakable mark of Dickens's writing". For instance, an important stage in Comrade Napoleon's gradual abandonment of the principles of animalism occurs when he sits down at table to eat. But in relating this, Orwell tells just a little bit more; he "always ate," he tells us, "from the crown Derby dinner service which had been in the glass cupboard in the drawing room." This comic surface of the prose is the major effect of *Animal Farm*. The book is, in fact, a piece of literary self-indulgence. As a writer Orwell has here taken refuge in a simple, comfortable Edwardian form which allows him a perspective upon the modern world and a relationship with his reader which, however relaxed they may be, are neither engaging nor illuminating.

Yet however slight *Animal Farm* may be in itself, it is extremely interesting as a prelude to Orwell's last and most considerable work of fiction *Nineteen Eighty-Four*. For in his final book Orwell further exploits the realisation that had come to him in the conception and the writing of its predecessor: that his way of seeing the world could best be expressed in those literary forms characteristic of Edwardian England and with which he had for so long been familiar. If the fables of Rudyard Kipling supplied the pattern for *Animal Farm*, in *Nineteen Eighty-Four* the models are the romances of H. G. Wells and, to a lesser extent, those of G. K. Chesterton. But the salient difference between the books is that the latter work treats of issues of experience that are vividly and often agonisingly alive to the writer. Unlike *Animal Farm*, *Nineteen Eighty-Four* is an attempt to confront and to express specifically and unrelentingly the nature of modern experience. Here Orwell uses the Edwardian form not in order to distance himself from the moral horrors of the Europe of the day, but rather as an anchor to lend himself stability in the charting of them. And as a work of literary art this attempt, despite its several and obvious imperfections, is a memorable one. The form of the Wellsian utopia is completely serviceable to Orwell's purposes, and by using it as a base he is able to make a sustained aesthetic statement in a way he had not been able to do during the thirties when he had experimented with other forms of fiction.

Nineteen Eighty-Four follows the standard pattern of the Wellsian scientific romance. It begins by presenting a human being who finds himself in a world that is to him and to the reader strange and inhuman. In Wells this world is remote either geographically or in time and the hero is transported thither either by mischance, as in *The Island of Dr. Moreau*, or by some strange and improbable contraption, as in *The Time Machine*, or by some peculiar psychic mechanism, as in *The Sleeper Awakes*.[70] Winston Smith, it is true, is not conveyed to the world of 1984; he has grown to manhood in that society and is a native there. Nevertheless, though in that world, Winston Smith, we are asked to believe, is not of it. Like Wells's heroes, Winston Smith is a representative of his author's and his reader's world. And in the opening chapters of *Nineteen Eighty-Four*, as in those of Wells's books, the reader comes, through the hero, to experience shock, horror and bewilderment at the remote world that is portrayed. And with the hero, he comes more and more to desire some explanation of the situation with which he had been confronted. In the scientific romance it is customary for this desire to be satisfied about half-way through when the suspense is relieved and the hero at last encounters some figure with power and information who explains the mystifying world to him. In this regard Winston's long conversations in the torture chamber with the Inner Party member O'Brien serve the same narrative purpose as, for instance, Prendrick's conversations with Dr. Moreau. The second section of a scientific romance, in which the hero is made fully cognisant of the barbarousness around him, is usually

70 *The Sleeper Awakes*, "a vision of a glittering, sinister world", as he called it, seems to have made an especially strong impression on Orwell. He once wrote, "Everyone who has ever read *The Sleeper Awakes* remembers it." "Prophecies" in *Tribune*, 12 July, 1940, pp. 16, 17.

followed by a third in which the story line is resumed. The narrative climax comes with the hero's usually unsuccessful attempt to resist, to escape, or at least to preserve his humanity in the face of the horrors around him.

Understandably, this particular species of prose fiction was attractive to Orwell. For it makes possible, in a way that the form of fiction which we think of as the novel does not, a synthesis of Orwell's usually irreconcilable purposes as a writer; the making of didactic proposals for individual and social renewal, and the creation of literary art. As an art form the scientific romance is perfectly amenable to two distinctively modern preoccupations: the collapse of civilisation and the process whereby man is dehumanised. And if we can agree with Bernard Bergonzi's thesis in *The Early H. G. Wells*, we will be able to recognise as achieved works of art Wells's treatment of these themes in some of his scientific romances. A further example of the aesthetic possibilities of the form, and one of which Orwell was aware, is Fyodor Zamyatin's *We*, which, in translation at least, is a work of great subtlety and delicacy.[71] Nevertheless, despite this proven potential as art the scientific romance has been used traditionally and most frequently as a form of *Tendenzliteratur*, as a vehicle for writers who have wished to educate, even to indoctrinate their readers. Given this purpose, the vision of the future that characterises the form serves to demonstrate, and usually in a horrifying way, the sort of society that will sooner or later come into being if certain tendencies in the present are not halted. Furthermore, when it is used for purposes of propaganda the form is very likely to contain an element of satire. Its warning about the future can entail not only criticism but also mockery of the present, and the horrors to come may be there not only as prophecy, but as a way of teasing the reader out of his complacency.[72] Such propagandist

[71] For some comments on the similarities between *We* and *Nineteen Eighty-Four* see *Zamyatin, A Soviet Heretic* by D. T. Richards (London, 1962). Mr. Richards also establishes Zamyatin's interest in Wells and maintains that his "two articles on Wells must stand high in all the literature on the English writer."

[72] It should be noted that these remarks refer only to modern examples of the form. It is, of course, a fact that certain nineteenth-century scientific romances provided visions of the future which

satire is present in Wells's *The Sea Raiders, The Empire of the Ants* and in many of his later romances. And of course the satiric element is even more prominent in that other famous example of the form which Orwell had read, Aldous Huxley's *Brave New World*.

A peculiarly brutal and harrowing satiric propaganda is the most salient feature of *Nineteen Eighty-Four*. Indeed, it is this that accounts for the great fame of the book. Its very title has become a household word and the frightening vision of the future which it retails is an item in the consciousness of every literate person. And this, it would seem, because Orwell the satirist has succeeded most tellingly in objectifying the very worst fears of his time. Obviously, for those who had lived through the years of Fascism and Stalinism, Orwell's totalitarian state of Oceania, with its slave proletariat ruled by the "the Party" and a leader such as Big Brother, was a terrifying possibility which easily recommended itself. And to those who had twice known total war on a global scale, the prospect of unending warfare between vast superstates, as presented in *Nineteen Eighty-Four*, was similarly plausible. Frighteningly familiar also were the actualities of day to day life as Orwell envisions them: the Thought Police, the torture chambers, the doctrine of "double think", the subordination of familial and sexual feeling to party loyalty, the betrayals, the frenzied political gatherings in which mass hatred is continually redirected in accordance with the party line. Above all, and this accounts for the fact that the book still continues as a reference point in our thinking even though its specifically political prophecy may no longer seem convincing, there is the picture of a man manipulated physically and mentally by an omnipotent and unchallengeable social system. Deprived of all physical privacy by the two way telescreen and the hovering aircraft of the Thought Police and of his mental freedom by unrelenting propaganda, Oceanic man is either a witless prole who can be ignored, or a completely conditioned party member. And if, like Winston Smith, he resists the system,

---

their authors commended, visions which were intended to inspire ambition, initiative and effort in readers. For a very detailed account of the history and the characteristics of the form, see Richard Gerber, *Utopian Fantasy* (London, 1955).

if in 1984 he tries to live in terms of the normal humanity of 1948, then he is doomed to be refashioned through mental and physical torture so as to adhere to the party doctrines and love Big Brother.

These then are some of the well known images of the future to be found in *Nineteen Eighty-Four*. They are, of course, only a part of what the book contains, and extrapolated from the work as they usually are, they make for a distorted idea of it. And it is unfortunate that this agonising cautionary tale should have come to overshadow the more creative literary intention that can be discerned in the book. In themselves the projections have but slight literary interest. They are not what in Coleridgean terms could be called works of imagination; they are at the very best works of fancy. Yet even in terms of this latter category and in terms more particularly of the satiric fancy which, as we have seen, the scientific romance permits and encourages the propagandist to indulge, *Nineteen Eighty-Four* is often crude and unsatisfactory. In fact so glaring is the lack of control in some of the satiric and propagandist sections that serious damage is done to the overall effect of the book.

The tonal variations in Orwell's satire are few. Basically it is a matter of just two standard attitudes. First there is the controlled, fluent and unhesitating straightforwardness with which he describes the inordinately preposterous. Here, for instance, is how this manner obtrudes with a skilfully managed incidentalness in a description of Julia, the girl with whom Winston, against all Party rules, has an affair:

> As she came nearer he saw that her right arm was in a sling, not noticeable at a distance because it was of the same colour as her overalls. Probably she had crushed her hand while swinging round one of the big kaleidoscopes on which the plots of novels were roughed in. It was a common accident in the Fiction department.

Taken alone the manner of this is unobjectionable, but when so many of the institutions of Oceania are presented in this way, it becomes monotonous and the joke loses its effect. And, of course, the matter itself is finally too trivial, too unengaging for memorable satire. Instead of feeling teased, shocked or scandalised, we experience merely a rather flippant interest in the plausibility of Orwell's ingeniousness.

The alternative satiric manner in *Nineteen Eighty-Four* is even more damagingly unsatisfactory. This is the satire that is charged with powerful emotion, the emotion that Irving Howe characterised when he observed that "the book trembles with an eschatological fury."[73] It is a deep anger and disgust elicited above all by the barbarous cruelty and inhumanity which Orwell envisions in his world of the future. Two good examples of it are to be found in the descriptions of the air raid and of Winston's night in the prison cell after being captured by the Thought Police. The effect of such scenes is very powerful; it is hard to forget either the sordid indignities they present or the feeling of revulsion they elicit. And yet at the same time, the reader cannot but resent being made to respond in this way. The satirist, it is true, has every right to affect the emotions of his reader, but only so long as this is done in the service of his satiric purpose, that is to say, for the sake of communicating a moral insight or awareness. But in these scenes, this is not the case. Here the assault on the reader's feelings is merely wanton. We do not need all the relentless detail of the prison scene, for instance, in order to experience very vividly the barbarism of a totalitarian society. Too much of the horrific in these scenes is redundant. It is as though Orwell is mesmerised by his own deep and bitter disgust. And the disgust influences unduly and objectionably his narrative control. This undisciplined preoccupation with horror explains why *Nineteen Eighty-Four* leaves such an impression of unpleasantness in our minds and why it is not pleasurable to contemplate a re-reading of the book. As a work of satiric propaganda, *Nineteen Eighty-Four* enjoys a reputation which bears little relation to its merit. Private obsessions have impaired Orwell's function in the public role of propagandist. His manner of setting down his warning is too uncontrolled; his satire is at times too thin and at other times too intense.

But even as propaganda, the book is more complex than the current account of it would suggest. Orwell is not just concerned to give us a vivid portrayal of what life would be like in a totalitarian society. He also addresses himself to the more difficult problem of defining the totalitarian mind. He is con-

[73] Irving Howe, "Orwell: History as Nightmare" in *Politics and the Novel* (London, 1961), p. 236.

cerned to provide some critical description of the psychological state within the individual which makes the totalitarian state possible. And his gruesome pictures of the future are really a device for enlarging and illuminating certain mental and emotional attitudes that were observable to him in the present. Orwell is unhesitating in his account of the origin of the totalitarian impulse. He locates it in certain distortions in the intellectual life. The party which rules Oceania is made up of intellectuals, intellectuals in the broad sense of the word suggested in the essay "England Your England" where Orwell lists "the people who are most at home in and most definitely of the modern world, the technicians and the higher paid skilled workers, the airmen and their mechanics, the radio experts, film producers, popular journalists and industrial chemists." Such people, it is true, are just members of the Outer Party, the mere instruments of policy. For an understanding of the actual philosophy upon which both party and state are based we are referred to the Inner Party, which is composed of intellectuals in the narrower sense of the word, men concerned with the propounding of a political and social and cultural philosophy. Orwell's purpose is to attack this philosophy and also the state of mind that nourishes it. In fact his most serious propagandist purpose in *Nineteen Eighty-Four* is his last and most thought out and most energetic assault on the very thing that had preoccupied him throughout the thirties, namely the perilous derangement of the intellectual life. The Inner Party member O'Brien is clearly recognisable as the representation of everything that Orwell in his essays had objected to in modern intellectuals. He is, in fact, Orwell's image of the totalitarian mind at its worst, and also at its most articulate.

The most detailed characterisation of O'Brien occurs in the scenes where he endeavours through argument and torture to make Winston accept the teachings of the Party. In these pages he is often referred to as an inquisitor or as a priest. And the Catholic if not the Irish associations of his name are presumably intended to emphasise this role. His main purpose as Winston Smith's grand inquisitor is to destroy Smith's moral and intellectual autonomy and to establish in its place a slavish, unreflecting adherence to the continually changing and contradictory view of the Party about what is false and true, real and unreal. This is his argument:

> "Only the disciplined mind can see reality, Winston. You believe that reality is something objective, external, existing in its own right. You also believe that the nature of reality is self-evident. When you delude yourself into thinking you see something, you assume that everyone else sees the same thing as you. But I tell you, Winston, that reality is not external. Reality exists in the human mind and nowhere else. Not in the individual mind, which can make mistakes, and in any case soon perishes; only in the mind of the Party, which is collective and immortal."

The tone of this justification of the subjection of the individual is philosophical; the words are calm and logical. Only as O'Brien moves on to describe the process whereby the Party converts the heretic do we sense the particular impulse of feeling behind them. At this point, we scarcely need to be told that O'Brien's face "was filled with a sort of exaltation, a lunatic intensity." For the rhythm of his words and the gloating cruelty which they convey suggest the distorted emotions that are at work:

> "When you finally surrender to us, it must be of your own free will. We do not destroy the heretic because he resists us; so long as he resists us we never destroy him. We convert him, we capture his inner mind, we reshape him. We burn all evil out of him; we bring him over to our side, not in appearance, but genuinely, heart and soul."

The joy in having "power over" which is so patent in these words is the next topic to which O'Brien addresses himself. Here at last we are given an explanation of his deepest motives, of the *raison d'être* of the Party and the social order which it has created and also, in terms of Orwell's propagandist intention, the "why" of totalitarianism generally. The fundamental purpose of the Party, O'Brien explains, is the cult of power, power for its own sake, as an end not as a means. "God is power" and the members of the Party are "the priests of power". The Party, he implies, is a communion of those devoted to experiencing the sensation of power, something which is achieved through the very act of dominating others. "Power," says O'Brien, "is in

157

inflicting pain and humiliation." "Power," he goes on in words that are reminiscent of Dr. Moreau, "is in tearing human minds to pieces and putting them together in new shapes of your own choosing." For this sadistic sensation the Party works to control and to reduce human consciousness. "In our world," says O'Brien, "there will be no emotions except fear, rage, triumph and self-abasement. Everything else we shall destroy—everything. . . . There will be no art, no literature, no science." "But always," he goes on, "there will be the intoxication of power, constantly increasing and constantly growing subtler." O'Brien concludes this phase of his explanation with an image which serves to make vivid the unmitigated atrocity of the cult of power. "If you want a picture of the future," he says, "imagine a boot stamping on a human face—forever." In the essay "Raffles and Miss Blandish", first published in 1944, Orwell, we remember, remarked that "The interconnection between sadism, masochism, success-worship, power-worship and totalitarianism is a huge subject whose edges have barely been scratched, and even to mention it is considered somewhat indelicate." In *Nineteen Eighty-Four* and particularly in these words of O'Brien we have Orwell's most sustained effort to do more than "scratch the edge" of the issue. In them we have the distillation of all his long meditations upon what he regarded as the evil peculiarly inherent in modern life.

In some of the many essays of the forties in which Orwell broaches this modern obsession with power, the word which (with some irony) he uses to refer to it is "realism". "Realism" is the evil to which intellectuals are particularly susceptible. "The growth of 'realism'," he observes in the essay on Miss Blandish, "has been the great feature of the intellectual history of our own age." It seems very likely that Orwell's awareness of the charge of indelicacy likely to greet any attempt to investigate the phenomenon comes from his realisation that it would entail a most damaging criticism of the contemporary intellectual community. (The statement that 'even to mention it is considered somewhat indelicate" recalls passages in other essays which suggest friction between Orwell and the intellectual orthodoxy.) Certainly it is not difficult to discern in *Nineteen Eighty-Four* a projection and a criticism of the tendencies of the specifically literary orthodoxy of the time. For it is not fanciful, I think, to remark upon the ways in which O'Brien appears to serve as a caricature of certain symbolist attitudes. His cruelly contemptuous relegation to the status of mere "proles" of all those who are unable to participate in the community of a life-hating sensibility is itself a striking reminder of Axel's disdainful dismissal of the servants who will do the mere living for us. O'Brien's very manner and appearance also seem to be significant in this regard. For in a way which reminds us of one of the most characteristic of symbolist claims, O'Brien, in the early chapters of the book, gives the impression of referring back to an older and more civilised order. "He had," we are told, "a trick of resettling his spectacles on his nose which was curiously disarming—in some indefinable way, curiously civilised. It was a gesture which, if any one had still thought in such terms, might have recalled an eighteenth century nobleman offering his snuff-box." Nevertheless, long before the end of the book Orwell makes it clear that this aristocratic urbanity is but a mask concealing a crazed desire for hierarchy and power. Even the architecture of the four Party ministries (in one of which, the Ministry of Love, O'Brien officiates) suggests the same sort of inhuman aloofness, the same withdrawal from mere life that Axel's Castle has come to represent. The Ministry, we are told, is "an enormous pyramidal structure of glittering white concrete, soaring up, terrace after terrace, three hundred metres into the air". The implication of these details is also corroborated by O'Brien's own views as they are expressed in conversation with Winston Smith. For his stress upon consciousness as reality ("Reality is in the human mind and nowhere else"), his belief in the necessary subordination of the individual mind to some larger mind, his preoccupation with certain types of feeling and his cultivation of moments of memorable sensation are all part of what is to the student of modern literature a familiar pattern. And in these terms the Party itself, since it is a community of sensibility, may be seen to suggest the literary hegemony of the day. The party is, of course, a community that is united by its cultivation of the subtlest sensations of hierarchy and contempt. And it seems likely that this is an aspect of the modern literary orthodoxy that Orwell intended to attack. I should make it clear that I do not wish to claim that the propaganda in *Nineteen Eighty-Four* is directed exclusively or even principally against the symbolist culture of the time. It is no more this than it is an attack upon socialism or Roman Catholicism. O'Brien is more than a caricature of the symbolist mind. He is, above all, the embodiment of the peculiarly modern cult of power and hierarchy, the embodiment of a state of mind of which certain ideas of art, society and religion are but the functions. At its subtlest the propaganda in *Nineteen Eighty-Four* is a critical account of the unhygienic emotion and the distorted thinking which Orwell sees informing the intellectual life generally. And his campaign is against the cult of power sensation, the desire to control and reduce life which finds its representation in O'Brien and which expresses itself not only in political and religious and cultural terms but in every mode of contemporary thought. This is the basic object of Orwell's attack, and this is the evil which sets in motion all the more famous if less subtle horrors of 1984.

But this particular form of decadence and its attendant horrors serve as more than the targets of a propagandist attack. And Winston Smith himself is more than the unparticularised human being who serves as a standard item in a scientific romance. In one respect he is, to be sure, our man in a world that is not, but could be, ours. In one way he is our possible future fate. But he is also very much more than this. He is a character whose life and mind and temperament are elaborated upon by his author at great length and in great detail for their own sakes and certainly far beyond the requirements of the scientific romance. We are compelled to see him as a character in a novel and at the same time to see *Nineteen Eighty-Four* as a work of literary art. For despite the current and popular estimate of the book, it was not the propagandist but rather the aesthetic potential of the scientific romance which engaged Orwell's finest creative energy. And what is most valuable and important in the book are not its implied admonitions but rather its treatment of some of the issues of experience with which the art of fiction has traditionally been concerned: the nature of reality, the proper ordering of human relationships, the processes of society and the rendering and evaluating of feeling.

Regarded from this perspective, all the notorious barbarisms described in the book appear less as possible phenomena in the external world and more as objects in the hero's psychological landscape. And when we recall that surrealism was one of the major events of the intellectual history of the thirties in England, we find ourselves provided with a useful preliminary definition of the particular quality of *Nineteen Eighty-Four* as a novel. It contains a greater awareness of gross brutality than, say, the novels of Franz Kafka or of Kafka's English follower Rex Warner, but it resembles them in its manner of evoking a psychological hell. I hasten to add that I am not here trying to establish some exotic category for the book. I wish merely to take advantage of one that is historically handy. Surrealism is, after all, but one short-lived emphasis within the general symbolist tradition. And with all its particularities *Nineteen Eighty-Four* is in its general themes very representative of twentieth-century literary art in general. It is, at its simplest, the story of a man seeking to attain a full and properly human life in a social and intellectual context that is unpropitious.

It is also a story which, in its general outline, is autobiographical, treating as it does the dilemma of an intellectual (though not an "Inner Party" intellectual) who seeks to resist the hysterical totalitarianism to which his fellows have gone over by, among other things, seeking a revitalising contact with the common people, the proles. Like Orwell, Winston Smith does not succeed in making this contact, though like his author he continues to have faith in them as a source of regeneration. "The proles had stayed human. They had not become hardened inside. They had held on to the primitive emotions which he himself had had to relearn by conscious effort." Winston Smith tries other methods to rekindle the human feeling that he senses within him and that is associated with blurred memories of the old pre-totalitarian society. But none of these endeavours are ultimately successful. His attempt to subvert the system is quickly detected, as is his love affair with Julia, which is also an act of rebellion against the established order. And his most determined attempt to sustain some human feeling within himself by cultivating his memories and dreams of a more civilised past is also eventually frustrated when after intense mental and physical torture, he at last surrenders his consciousness to the party. Nevertheless, it is this feature of Winston's life, his attempt to achieve vital renewal, with which Orwell the novelist is most concerned. The book is, most importantly, the story of a man who cannot find vital sustenance in, or even accept as real, the reality of the world around him and who is compelled to search for reality within himself. Reality for Winston Smith is to be found, if it is to be found at all, in his own individual consciousness, in his own reveries, dreams and memories of an older order. The plot of the novel, the sequence of events in the external world in which Winston participates, serves but to prove that here is no acceptable, no human reality. The plot thus reinforces the central theme of the book, which is Winston's search to find regeneration in terms of an enforced introversion. And what the book as a work of art has to offer us is a rendering of the painful actualities of this quest.

Here, of course, we have a tremendous paradox. For the Orwell who throughout his writing career had consciously sought to affirm the possibility of new social relationships and who in this self-same book in his depiction of O'Brien had implied some angry criticism of the symbolist position is here himself writing in effect as a symbolist. *Nineteen Eight-Four* is a novel which assumes and analyses consciousness as reality, and a work of art which offers us not a readily decipherable message but the very sensations of a man struggling to resist the dehumanising effect of the world around him and to attain that fuller state of being which he senses only within himself. In *Nineteen Eighty-Four*, as much as in *Four Quartets*, we are invited to assist at the processes of a man's consciousness as it struggles to experience a deeper order and meaning in life than contact with the phenomenal world will allow. I do not here intend any qualitative comparison between these two works; I merely wish to point out the similarity between them in essential subject matter in order to reinforce the point that in *Nineteen Eighty-Four* we have one of the belated works of symbolism. The book is in fact a rendering of that state of despair which Orwell had first broached in his discussion of Henry Miller and the surreal in the essay "Inside the Whale".

Orwell's method of evoking the various phases of Winston Smith's consciousness is often reminiscent of other symbolist works. The very first sentence of the novel brings with it some very distinct and recognisable echoes: "It was a bright cold day in April, and the clocks were striking thirteen." Later on the use of the twenty-four hour clock, like the Oceanic use of the decimal system and a dollar currency, will come to be just one of the ways in which the England of 1984 differs from the homely, more familiar and less regimented England of the past. But in this opening sentence it serves to introduce the atmosphere of the strange and the surreal which pervades the whole book. And of course the particular seasonal setting established in this sentence reminds us immediately of the most famous of symbolist poems in English, in which April brings neither spiritual nor physical rebirth but merely surreal and grotesque visions of living death. Both *The Waste Land* and *Nineteen Eighty-Four* deal in their different ways with the same essential experience, the sense of inhabiting some shabby no-man's land half-way between life and death. Winston Smith's perambulations through the streets of his unreal city in the early chapters of the novel, in a directionless quest for emotional and spiritual renewal, are reminiscent of those of Tiresias, and also of those of Dedalus and Bloom. And for Winston Smith, as for Tiresias, the shabby desuetude of the London townscape serves as the counterpart of his own interrogative despair:

> Were there always these vistas of rotting nineteenth-century houses, their sides shored up with balks of timber, their windows patched with cardboard and their roofs with corrugated iron, their crazy garden walls sagging in all directions? And the bombed sites where the plaster dust swirled in the air and the willow herb straggled over the heaps of rubble; and the places where the bombs had cleared a larger path and there had sprung up sordid colonies of wooden dwellings like chicken houses?

This apprehension of the unreal city recurs throughout the book:

> He seemed to see a vision of London vast and ruinous, city of a

million dustbins, and mixed up with it was a picture of Mrs. Parsons, a woman with a lined face and wispy hair, fiddling helplessly with a blocked wastepipe.

He felt as though he were wandering in the forests of the sea bottom, lost in a monstrous world where he himself was the monster. He was alone. The past was dead, the future unimaginable.

The chief narrative concern of the novel is with Winston's several endeavours to find release from this desolating isolation and unreality. It is also the story of his final and terrible realisation that from the outset his spiritual resources have been too slight to achieve this. Looking back over the novel as a whole we see this ultimate insight hinted at in the very moment when Winston makes his decision to seek for renewal. "He had accepted it. The end was contained in the beginning. But it was frightening; or more exactly, it was like a pretaste of death, like being a little less alive. . . . He had the sensation of stepping into the dampness of a grave . . . ." At the deepest level Winston's final defeat lies not in his discovery and torture by the Thought Police but in his realisation of the porousness of his own mind and will. That which he had hated in the external world is, he comes eventually to see, also at work within himself. Even his very best impulses are but disguises for it. And the special agony which is the main subject of the novel is the rending sense of the deludedness of all aspirations for renewal which suddenly comes to Winston Smith after a period of apparent spiritual and emotional progress.

In order to suggest something of the power of this ultimate vision, it is necessary first to establish the story of the quest for regeneration which forms its context. Winston Smith's first step in seeking to escape the *ennui* that possesses him at the beginning of the novel occurs when in one of his wanderings through the older and "prole" sections of London, he discovers Mr. Charrington's junk shop. Here he finds an assortment of old objects which belong to, and in some tenuous way resurrect for him, the dead past, "the vanished romantic past, the olden time as he liked to call it in his secret thoughts". From Mr. Charrington he buys the old diary which will serve him as a device for expressing his own true thoughts and feelings. This is his first major act of rebellion against the callously inhuman categories of perception enforced by the Party. Mr. Charrington himself, "a man of perhaps sixty, frail and bowed, with a long, benevolent nose, and mild eyes distorted by thick spectacles" and with "a vague air of intellectuality, as though he had been some kind of literary man, or perhaps a musician", also serves to encourage Winston in his quest for knowledge of the past. It is he who recalls for Winston the first two lines of the rhyme "Oranges and Lemons" which becomes an important motif both in Winston's consciousness and in the novel. Winston's gradual accumulation, line by line, of a knowledge of the rhyme accompanies and helps to suggest the expansion and renewal of his consciousness. The rhyme is for him an entry into the lost civilisation of the past. "It was curious, but when you said it to yourself you had the illusion of actually hearing bells, the bells of a lost London that still existed somewhere or other, disguised and forgotten. From one ghostly steeple after another he seemed to hear them pealing forth. Yet so far as he could remember, he had never in real life heard church bells ringing." Winston's subsequent efforts to try and recapture the lost lines of the rhyme is one of the ways in which Orwell conveys Winston's struggle to regain his lost human heritage. As a fictional technique for suggesting a particular type of mental struggle to recover the forgotten it works most successfully.

But Winston Smith's progress towards emotional renewal involves more than this search for contact with the civilisation of the past. It also entails a growing insight into and understanding of his own self, a process which is presented in terms of a continuing interior monologue that is made up of thoughts, responses, reflections, memories, dreams and also of the entries that Winston makes in his diary. In the opening chapters of the book, the diary is the most conspicuous method by which Winston gives expression to his feelings without forcing and distorting them to conform to the Party orthodoxy. As he writes in the diary, Winston is carried away by a new intensity in his emotions now they are allowed to go unchecked. "Suddenly he began writing in sheer panic, only imperfectly aware of what he was setting down." "He discovered that while he sat helplessly musing, he had also been writing as though by automatic action." In this way (a way, incidentally, that recalls the creative process as defined by the surrealists) Winston Smith learns to express the impulses of that deeper, unconscious self which the Party, for its own ends, seeks to repress. From this act of writing he gains his first awareness of himself as an individual human being. Most importantly, (for in terms of his spiritual rehabilitation it is more productive than his expressions of hysterical hatred of Big Brother, the symbol of the Party) he succeeds in putting down one of the reasons for his own self-loathing and disgust. This is the torturing memory of his experience with the prostitute in the proletarian section of London. Estranged from his wife Katharine who, from temperament as much as conviction, adheres strictly to the Party view that sexual relations are tolerable only for the purposes of propagation, Winston accepts the invitation of a prostitute he meets and goes with her to her house. When he first sees her she appears attractive. "She had a young face, painted very thick. It was really the paint that appealed to me, the whiteness of it, like a mask and the bright red lips." But when he is alone with her, he is appalled by her ghastly ugliness. "The paint was plastered so thick on her face that it looked as though it might crack like a cardboard mask. There were streaks of white in her hair; but the truly dreadful detail was that her mouth had fallen a little open, revealing nothing except a cavernous blackness. She had no teeth at all. . . . When I saw her in the light she was quite an old woman, fifty years old at least. But I went ahead and did it just the same." This memory of the cadaverous old woman with the face that is a painted mask is the first of his subconscious motives for a disgusted and dehumanising hatred of life that Winston, through the act of self-expression, is able to raise into his consciousness. His exorcising of this painful image is further aided by his subsequent love affair with Julia, which brings him the experience of sexual relationship as something joyful and exhilarating and completely different from the two other possibilities represented by Katharine and the old woman.

As a consequence of the emotional rebirth that accompanies his love for Julia, Winston also becomes able to bring into consciousness less accessible, less well defined images of guilt and pain. The movement of Winston's consciousness, as Orwell presents it, is a continuing alternation between perceptions and responses in the present and the memories which they call up from the past. Sometimes this is managed rather crudely by using the flashback; on other occasions, however, memories are shown emerging more naturally into Winston's consciousness, sometimes as a result of the action of the involuntary memory, which as a literary device Orwell now employs more subtly than he had done ten years earlier in *Coming Up for Air*. One of Winston's most obsessive and most disturbing memories comes to him in dreams. It concerns the disappearance of his mother and sister (they are assumed to have been killed or sent to a forced labour camp) which occurred when Winston himself was still a child. In his dreams Winston sees them in a surreal and continually changing dream situation:

> They were down in some subterranean place—the bottom of a well, for instance, or a very deep grave—but it was a place which, already far below him, was itself moving downwards. They were in the saloon of a sinking ship looking up at him through the darkening water. There was still air in the saloon, they could still see him and he them, but all the while they were sinking down, down into the green waters which in another moment must hide them from his sight for ever. He was out in the light and air while they were being sucked down to death, and they were down there *because* he was up here. He knew it and they knew it and he could see the knowledge in their faces.

The guilt to which this memory attests, "a memory that he must have deliberately pushed out of his consciousness over many years", is only fully understood during Winston's time of intense happiness with Julia. On one of their meetings Julia brings a bar of chocolate of the kind no longer generally available in Oceania. For Winston the chocolate recalls a memory of the past: "The first whiff of its scent had stirred up some memory which he could not pin down, but which was powerful and troubling." "The taste was delightful. But there was still that memory moving round the edges of his consciousness, something strongly felt but not reducible to definite shape, like an object seen out of the corner of one's eye." Sometime later, in a dream, the full outline and details of the memory become clear and reveal the origin of Winston's frightening sense of guilt towards his mother and sister. In his dream Winston relives his last day with them. Particularly he remembers how in his hunger he had nagged his mother for more than his due share of their very meagre ration of chocolate. Having eaten his own and his mother's portion, he had snatched the small piece remaining from the hands of his baby sister. As the child cries, Winston runs from the house. When he returns, his mother and sister have already been taken away, and he never sees them again.

This sudden and full awareness and acceptance of guilt is one of the ways in which, through his association with Julia, Winston is able to cure his emotional sickness. For this recognition of guilt brings with it a recognition of a standard of value by which the guilt is known. And this value is also there in the dream; it is represented by the gesture with which, after Winston had snatched the chocolate, his mother had clasped the weeping, frightened child to her. Winston now sees this gesture as representing something that is virtually extinct in Oceania, namely the spontaneous and uncalculated and completely natural expression of human feeling. "It would not have occurred to her that an action which is ineffectual thereby becomes meaningless. If you loved someone, you loved him, and when you had nothing else to give, you still gave love. When the last of the chocolate was gone, his mother had clasped the child in her arms. It was no use, it changed nothing, it did not produce more chocolate, it did not avert the child's death or her own; but it seemed natural to her to do it." The dream, in fact, recalls to Winston's mind a possibility in experience that is denied by the present way of life. "Such things, he saw, could not happen today. Today there were fear, hatred and pain, but no dignity of emotion, no deep or complex sorrows. All this he seemed to see in the large eyes of his mother and his sister looking up at him through the green water, hundreds of fathoms down and still sinking."

For Winston, to know his guilt is also to recognise and to be enriched by a completely new sense of the possibilities of human feeling and relationships. He now has the strength and the courage to recover this knowledge from the past because of the regenerative influence of his relationship with Julia. His love for her is the highest point of his spiritual and emotional rehabilitation. It marks his closest approach to a full and mature humanity before he is struck down. As narrative the love affair is rather commonplace. And this is not just because it is a celebration of "ordinary" love against a social background where such love is impossible. Rather it is because Orwell is able to offer only certain set and very rudimentary love situations; early antagonisms, a declaration, furtive meetings, the joyful coming together in the countryside and then the regular meetings in the room above Mr. Charrington's shop. In many ways the story strikes us as a reworking of the same experience described in *Keep the Aspidistra Flying*, though here embellished with digressions on the Party's proscription of all sexual relationships based on love. Nor is Julia herself very interesting as a character. She is not a realised human being, but some sort of representative of femininity. ("With Julia, everything came back to her own sexuality.") However, all this amounts to is a practical skill and cunning at conforming externally to the dictates of the party while privately following her own inclinations. But the triteness of the characterisation of Julia and indeed of the whole love situation is no great defect in the novel. For Orwell's emphasis is not upon the love story as such but rather upon the history of a human consciousness as it seeks expansion and enrichment, a general process of which the love experience is but a part. And if Orwell is not altogether successful at relating a story of love, he does succeed in his attempt to evoke the experience and sensation of love as a part and phase of his hero's mind.

One of the ways in which Orwell accomplishes this essentially symbolist undertaking is through a skilful use of the device which is, of all devices, the most appropriate—the symbol itself. And by examining the major symbol of the novel it is possible to suggest the particular and delicate states of consciousness which the love experience evokes. The symbol is the paperweight which Winston buys from Mr. Charrington. It is a large lump of glass shaped like a hemisphere with a piece of pink coral like a rose or sea anemone at the heart of it. "There was a peculiar softness as of rainwater, in both the colour and the texture of the glass." When Winston first sees this object, it is not only its beauty that interests and attracts him but also, as with the diary, "the air it seemed to possess of belonging to an age quite different from the present one". And his purchase of it constitutes a further act of rebellion against the life of the present. "It was a queer thing, even a compromising thing, for a Party member to have in his possession. Anything old, and for that matter anything beautiful, was always vaguely suspect." This is only the first of a whole complex of meanings that the object will come to hold for him. As he is returning to his flat after buying the paperweight, Winston Smith encounters Julia whom at this time he still regards as a member of the Thought Police, and one especially intent upon spying on him personally. In the panic and hatred which the sight of her inspires, Winston contemplates murdering the girl. The paperweight now loses its original significance for him and becomes just "a piece of glass" which "would be heavy enough for the job". The suggestion of the weakness and temporariness of Winston Smith's civilised perception reinforces our impression of the keen and intense cruelty to which, like his fellow citizens of Oceania, he himself is prone. Here is how Orwell presents Winston Smith's particular fear and hatred of Julia at the beginning of the novel: "Vivid, beautiful hallucinations flashed through his mind. He would flog her to death with a rubber truncheon. He would tie her naked to a stake and shoot her full of arrows like Saint Sebastian. He would ravish her and cut her throat at the moment of climax." This is but one expression of Winston's psychological sickness, a sickness which is reminiscent of that diagnosed by D. H. Lawrence in Gerald Crich in Women in Love, a character who also stands as a representative of the apocalyptic degeneration of civilised consciousness. It is a psychological sickness which has its physical counterpart in Winston's hacking cough and in the horrible varicose ulcer on his ankle.

Winston's return to health begins with Julia's declaration of love for him and with the surge of feeling within him that impels him to the adventure of meeting her. The sense of nervous desire which possesses Winston at the time of their first meeting in the countryside is finely managed. And so is the feeling of abandonment to sexual experience that marks the next phase of their relationship. This in turn is followed by a new stage in which "a deep tenderness, such as he had not felt for her before, suddenly took hold of him." "He wished that they were a married couple of ten years' standing." "He wished above all that they had some place where they could be alone together without feeling the obligation to make love every time they met." The desire for permanence in part induces Winston to take the risk of renting the room above Mr. Charrington's shop; though that action is also motivated by more complex feelings that are again represented by and conveyed in terms of the paperweight. "Actually the idea had first floated into his mind in the form of a vision of the glass paperweight mirrored by the surface of the gateleg table." The paperweight in its delicate colour and texture is a counterpart of the peculiar feeling which the relationship with Julia now signifies for Winston. "There was such a depth of it and yet it was almost as transparent as air. It was as though the surface of the glass had been the arch of the sky enclosing a tiny world with its atmosphere complete." "The paperweight was the room he was in and the coral was Julia's life and his own, fixed in a sort of eternity at the heart of the crystal." The paperweight has further significance. For at the same time as it serves to evoke the particular texture of Winston's feeling for Julia, it also suggests and relates to this those valuable feelings which in dream he is able to remember in his mother. For that dream "had all occured inside the glass paperweight, but the surface of the glass was the dome of the sky, and inside the dome everything was flooded with clear, soft light in which one could see into interminable distances."

To appreciate the complex of finely shaded feelings that attaches to the paperweight (and though Orwell may be accused of being at times too explicit about the symbol, it does nevertheless work successfully) is to experience with a memorable shock of horror the brutal destruction of them that comes with the narrative climax of the novel when Julia and Winston are at last discovered by the Thought Police. Just before this happens, Julia and Winston are looking down from the window of their room upon an old working woman hanging out clothes on a line. As she works she sings a popular song. Its words are trivial, but the singing of it is for Winston an expression of sane and healthy human feeling. And as he continues to look at the woman he finds in her a sort of beauty. The attitude to life registered here is the direct opposite of that suggested by the memory of the prostitute: "It had never before occured to him that the body of a woman of fifty, blown up to monstrous dimensions by child-bearing, then hardened, roughened by work till it was coarse in the grain like an over-ripe turnip, could be beautiful." This is the moment in which Winston Smith experiences his greatest love and reverence for life, a feeling which is expressed in words that remind us of those used to describe the paperweight and the dream. "The mystical reverence that he felt for her was somehow mixed up with the aspect of the pale cloudless sky, stretching away behind the chimney pots into interminable distances." As Julia and Winston listen to this song of life, they become wistfully conscious of the paucity and vulnerability of the vital experience which they have known together.

"We are the dead," he said.
"We are the dead," echoed Julia dutifully.

And then comes the terrible interruption: "'You are the dead,' said an iron voice behind them." Immediately the atmosphere of reverence and calm is rent by the cacophany of the official voice from the hidden telescreen, the iron shod boots on the stairs and the violent entry of the black uniformed men into the room. Amidst all the noise, Julia and Winston are brutally seized by the Thought Police. And then as the culmination of the horror: "There was another crash. Someone had picked up the glass paperweight from the table and smashed it to pieces on the hearthstone." Given the many associations of the paperweight, this is for the reader the most terrible sound in a scene that succeeds in conveying, primarily in auditory terms, the transition from a sense of quiet joy to one of stark horror.

From this moment the course of the novel is completely changed. It is no longer the story of a man's regeneration, but of his subjection and reduction. The renewal of life, it now turns out, is but part of the theme of *Nineteen Eighty-Four*. For to Orwell the quest for such renewal inevitably brings retribution at the hands of a society that is founded upon a hatred of life. The twentieth-century mind as it is represented by Winston Smith may try to move towards a more abundant life, but as a consequence of this action it is doomed also to experience a terrible retaliation from the inhuman and unliving social order around it. It is the experience of the sadistic destruction of a living consciousness that the remainder of the book is concerned to evoke. And if the full implications of Orwell's words are taken, the experience is one of a chilly, unfathomable horror.

For the worst agony of Winston's captivity lies not in the brainwashing techniques of the torture chamber, nor in the discovery that those who, like Mr. Charrington, appeared to represent a civilised humanity are in reality agents of the Party, nor in the thoroughgoing hatred and contempt for human life expressed by O'Brien. Worst of all is O'Brien's demonstration of the fallaciousness of Winston's belief in the impregnability and sovereignty of the individual human mind. Hitherto, Winston had believed in a man's ultimate freedom from the influences of the external world, a freedom which he had visualised as the privacy of "the few cubic centimeters inside your skull". With his imprisonment comes the realisation of the falsity of this idea. This realisation is rendered in such a way as to call in question the reality of all Winston Smith's previous experience. In this regard, it is very important to remember that Winston's first impulse to rebel against the Party had come to him in a dream that occurred seven years before the events related in the novel. "Seven years it must be—he had dreamed he was walking through a pitch-dark room. And someone sitting to one side of him had said as he passed: 'We shall meet in the place where there is no darkness.' It was said very quietly, almost casually— a statement, not a command." Henceforth, this dream with its promise of hope, friendship and a new awareness and illumination is one of the chief sources of Winston's willingness to resist the menacing sterility of the world around him. And so it is a keen and almost dementing agony for Winston to discover, as he does after his arrest, that his dream did not originate in his own mind. "And once—Winston could not remember whether it was in a drugged sleep, or in normal sleep, or even in a moment of wakefulness—a voice murmured in his ear: 'Don't worry, Winston; you are in my keeping. For seven years I have watched over you. Now the turning point has come. I shall save you. I shall make you perfect.' He was not sure whether it was O'Brien's voice; but it was the same voice that had said to him 'We shall meet in the place where there is no darkness' in that other dream, seven years ago." The dream, it is suggested, was not Winston's own, but something mysteriously planted in his consciousness by the Party in order to test his orthodoxy and loyalty. "He knew now that for seven years the Thought Police had watched him—like a beetle under a magnifying glass. There was no physical act, no word spoken aloud, that they had not noticed, no train of thought that they had not been able to infer." What is terrifying about this is not just the idea of an all powerful state able to infiltrate the very consciousness of the individual, either mystically (for that would seem to be the implication of the seven years) or through some special psychological technique. Even more perturbing is the realisation that the human mind can be secretly penetrated by the very forces which it wishes to resist, and that a man's best private impulses can be but disguises for the influence of the external environment which he consciously rejects. "The place where there is no darkness" is an important motif in the novel, and the awareness to which it eventually conduces is such as to make unreal the very sense of regeneration which Winston has known. And this, above all, is the particular agony which the third and final section of *Nineteen Eighty-Four* renders—that sense of the unreality of the self which is consequent upon a willed isolation and estrangement from the circumambient world. This is the most significant matter of the book, to which the more obvious and more sensational horrors and beatings and all the paraphernalia of the scientific romance are definitely secondary. It is a state of consciousness which can entail only a living death, a state of which the waste land of London is the image, that waste land in which just one year after the beginning of his search for salvation, Winston Smith again finds himself wandering "on a vile, biting day in March, when the earth was like iron and all the grass seemed dead and there was not a bud anywhere except a few crocuses which had pushed themselves up to be dismembered by the wind."

Orwell's evocation of the strange hallucinatory limbo to which the vital consciousness is condemned in the modern world is finely managed. And the only reason one can find to explain why the novel fails to enjoy recognition as a work of art is that its aesthetic effect is obscured and mitigated by the propaganda. There are too many long and elaborate descriptions of the details of Oceanic life which are all passages of secondary intensity. Too often both the hero and the movement of the novel are relegated while the author goes into an excessive and detailed account of, for instance, the status of the proles or the hierarchy of the Party. An especially glaring example of this sort of thing is the long extract from *The Theory and Practice of Oligarchical Collectivism* by Emmanuel Goldstein, the leader of the Brotherhood, supposedly the underground movement devoted to the overthrow of the Party. As an historical account of how Oceanic society came into being, the chapters quoted are of some interest as an essay on the possibilities of future history. But they do not allow themselves to be smoothly integrated into the development of the novel. Like the essay on "The Principles of Newspeak", and indeed like many of the passages that describe Oceanic institutions, the extracts from Goldstein's book seem better suited, as critics have often suggested, to an appendix. However, if they were thus removed, the propagandist functions of the book would obviously be greatly impaired. All of which leads us back to the proposition that in *Nineteen Eighty-Four* there are two not quite compatible purposes at work. All the elaborate inventiveness in the propaganda weakens the impact of the art. And at the same time the despair that is anatomised in the art deranges the propagandist prose in the unpleasant ways we have already noted. Nevertheless, despite this imperfection, *Nineteen Eighty-Four* is unquestionably Orwell's best novel. It reveals an engagement with the complexities of emotional experience that is not to be found in any of his other novels. And the particular *frisson* which is the chief effect of the book, the shock of horror at doubting the autonomy of the individual moral consciousness, remains one of the more memorable reading experiences in modern literature.

There is one further and final aspect of the book which is of special significance in terms of the approach to Orwell's writings that has been emphasised in this essay, and that is its very pronounced autobiographical element. We cannot but remark again that one of the things which the book involves is a recapitulation of the major experiences and phases of Orwell's own life. The story of Winston Smith is also very much a resumé of Orwell's own history. Thus in Winston Smith's act of rebellion, in his attempt to escape the dehumanising influences of his native environment, we have a representation of the major act of Orwell's own life. Smith's search for relationship and alliance with the oppressed is also his author's. And his slogan, "If there is hope it lies with the proles", is also obviously an expression of Orwell's own outlook during the thirties. Furthermore, neither character nor author has his faith easily shaken by the difficulties of making such contact. For both, the working class serves as the objectification of the good life, even if only in terms of images and memories. Both commit themselves to fight for the valuable feelings which these images evoke, and commit themselves to essays in constructive autobiography. And most important of all, author as well as character come at the very end to doubt these commitments and to feel forced to regard them as a futile, foredoomed and (most terrible of all) deluded lyricism.

Such an estimate can only seem shocking in the depth and intensity of its pessimism. This is because there is nothing in Orwell's preceding writings to prepare us for the vehemence of the despair in this final statement. And we are quick, perhaps anxious, to recall Orwell's own suggestion of the influence of illness on the writing of it. But even if we are able to some extent to regard the book as an aberration, as the expression of an only temporary state of mind, its inevitable effect is to make us view Orwell's history from a new perspective. Above all, it serves to remind us of the extreme precariousness of the Orwellian vision. We are made to recall that neither his idea of the egalitarian society nor his commitment to democratic feeling were easy to his nature and background. Both were created consciously and with difficulty. They were an ideal that was confirmed only on rare occasions by actual experience. His vision was not something innate; it was created by imagination and sustained by will and moral energy. And *Nineteen Eighty-Four* makes it all too clear how aware he was of the challenge to his commitments presented by that alternative view of life which was the more familiar one for the articulate consciousness of the time. Indeed, the book shows how Orwell was able, at moments at least, to become convinced of the inevitability of this more conventional set of feelings. The Orwellian commitment, the book suggests (and in view of the social nature of his commitments, this is the greatest of the many paradoxes in his life), cannot finally prevent the isolation, the solipsism, the despairing sense of unreality that constitute the standard version of the modern condition. *Nineteen Eighty-Four* is the most important evidence of the perpetual tension in Orwell's mind between two opposing attitudes to experience. It makes clear the continuing and obdurate difficulties involved in the commitment to George Orwell and the renunciation of Eric Blair. It shows the contradictions and the pain underlying the often bluff Orwellian persona. It emphasises the complexity of what was in modern times a rare moral endeavour.

The autobiographical significance of *Nineteen Eighty-Four* is not confined, however to Orwell's reasonably explicit retrospect upon his life. Implicit in the book is a further fact about his life which in terms of his whole career is equally surprising. I refer to the aesthetic achievement represented by the book, an achievement which in its underlying feeling as well as in its surface devices and techniques is essentially symbolist. This is another confirmation of Orwell's double awareness. It is an unconscious expression of the extent to which he continued to be influenced until the very end of his life by the orthodox categories of feeling and expression. During the thirties the orthodoxy never took complete possession of his mind. For the sake of modishness or as a result of his early uncertainty as a novelist, he had employed its techniques. But his incompatibility with the spirit behind them is shown by the fact that they appear as mere, though often disfiguring, excrescences upon his novels. Their very inappropriateness helps to reveal Orwell's true (and very traditional) purpose as a novelist, which was to describe social life and to identify the valuable in social terms. The symbolist aesthetic is, of course, totally irreconcilable with such intentions. And one interesting point about *Nineteen Eighty-Four* is that, especially when placed beside Orwell's earlier work, it illustrates this with abundant clarity. Only at the moment when he doubts the possibility of value in social terms, does he become fully susceptible to the standard modern forms. (This is not to say that at the end of his life Orwell consciously became a symbolist. Orwell the writer, like Winston Smith the man, succumbed to the pervasive and insinuating orthodoxy of the age in spite of himself.) If *Nineteen Eighty-Four* helps to characterise the nature of the symbolist mind, it is more important as a testimony to the extent of its power. For the final effect of the book is to remind us, in specifically literary terms, of the extreme difficulty of Orwell's twenty years of resistance to the contemporary orthodoxy. Even on those few occasions when his excursions in quest of valuable social experience were rewarded, he was always, we remember, tormented by doubts about his ability as a writer to do justice to the occasion. These difficulties must in great part be attributed to the fact that his endeavour could find no support from the literary methods of the age. Orwell's quest for new experience entailed a further problem of new forms. On the other hand, in his moment of doubt the age was with him; the forms were there, as they had always been, to recommend themselves. The literary aspect of the Orwellian struggle is made clear by the difference between *Homage to Catalonia* and *Nineteen Eighty-Four*. There is every reason to believe that the former represented the more profound emotional experience for Orwell. But it is the latter which is Orwell's most resonant and most memorable evocation of feeling. His most creative and original vision struggled awkwardly for expression; his moment of doubt was confirmed and specified by the pervasive categories of the time. And this we must conclude is the crucial part of Orwell's significance for us. As an artist and an autobiographer he provides us with a very rare perspective upon the relationship between modern feeling and modern art. If he is important as a critic of the modern orthodoxy, he is also important as a testimony to its power and, we might be prompted to say, to its inevitability. If the twenty years of Orwell's singular creative endeavour tell us something of the modern mind, so also in a different but complementary way does his final and most precipitous declension into despair.

INDEX